TOPICS IN APPLIED GEOGRAPHY

SLUM HOUSING AND
RESIDENTIAL RENEWAL

TOPICS IN APPLIED GEOGRAPHY
edited by Donald Davidson and John Dawson

titles published and in preparation
Slum housing and residential renewal
Soil erosion
Human adjustment to the flood hazard
Office location and public policy
Vegetation productivity
Government and agriculture
Soils and rural land use planning
Physical geography and economic development
  in the circumpolar North

D. A. Kirby
St David's University College
(University of Wales)
Lampeter

SLUM HOUSING AND RESIDENTIAL RENEWAL:
the case in urban Britain

Longman
London
and New York

Longman Group Limited London

*Associated companies, branches and representatives
throughout the world*

*Published in the United States of America
by Longman Inc., New York*

© D. A. Kirby 1979

First published 1979

British Library Cataloguing in Publication Data

Kirby, David A
  Slum housing and residential renewal. – (Topics in
  applied geography).
  1. Slums – Great Britain – History
  I. Title   II. Series
  301.5'4   HV4086

  ISBN 0-582-48691-2

Printed in Great Britain by
Richard Clay (Chaucer Press) Ltd.,
Bungay, Suffolk.

CONTENTS

List of tables   vii

Acknowledgements   viii

Introduction   ix

Section 1   **Review of theoretical and empirical research**   **1**

Chapter 1   Slums and the problem of slum housing   3
The nature of slums 3
The characteristics of slum dwellers 6
Attitudes of slum dwellers to moving 8
Conclusion: the problems of slums 10

Chapter 2   Obsolete housing and the problem of unfitness   13
Minimum fitness standards in England and Wales 14
Indexes of unfitness 16
Conclusion 23

Chapter 3   The process of obsolescence: the problem of changing life-styles   24
Concepts of housing obsolescence 24
The process of housing obsolescence 25
Conclusion 27

Chapter 4   The filtering concept and new building   29
The filtering process 29
Empirical studies of the filtering process 31
Conclusion 33

Chapter 5   Clearance and rebuilding   34
The impact of clearance 36
Personal and community disruption 40
Conclusion 46

Chapter 6   Housing rehabilitation   47
Social aspects 50
Economic aspects 51
Conclusion 56

Section 2   **Residential research in Britain**   **57**

Chapter 7   The slum problem in Britain   59
             The accuracy of the statistics   60
             Local authority estimates   60
             Independent estimates   61
             The nature of the standards   63
             Conclusion   65

Chapter 8   The policies of successive British Governments   69
             Pre-1930, the era of residential filtering   69
             1930–1969, the era of slum clearance   71
             1965 to the present, the era of rehabilitation   74
             Conclusion   76

Chapter 9   The achievements of successive British Governments   78
             Pre-1930   79
             1930–1965   80
             1965 to the present   82
             Conclusion   87

Chapter 10   Conclusion   89
             Slum eradication   89
             Reducing obsolescence   90

References   94
Index   99

LIST OF TABLES

2.1   Schedule of American Public Health Association.
2.2   Weights used in the Index of Decay.
2.3   Survey of Housing and Environmental Deficiency Index.
7.1   Size of slum clearance programmes for selected towns in England and Wales, 1933 and 1954 compared.
7.2   Unfit dwellings in England and Wales by type of area, 1967 and 1971 compared.
7.3   Unfit dwellings in England and Wales in 1971 by region, age and tenure.
9.1   Slum clearance programmes of local authorities, England and Wales, 1930–1939.
9.2   Slum clearance in England and Wales, 1954–1964.
9.3   Grant-aided improvements and conversions, England and Wales, 1949–1964.
9.4   Grant-aided improvements and conversions, England and Wales, 1965–1975.
9.5   Grants approved and characteristics of the dwelling stock by region, 1969–1975.
9.6   Slum clearance in England and Wales, 1965–1975.

ACKNOWLEDGEMENTS

Most of the text was written during a period of study leave from my position in the Department of Geography at Saint David's University College and I would like to express my gratitude to Professor David Thomas and the Senate for making this possible. My thanks must also go to my colleagues who undertook, most professionally, my duties during this period. Particular thanks are due to Dr John Dawson, series editior, for his initial stimulus and constructive comments on the manuscript and to Mrs Margaret Walker for her so rapid and accurate typing services. Mention must also be made of Iain Stevenson and the Editorial Staff at Longman. Their friendship and efficiency was most reassuring. The slum dwellers of Merseyside and Tyneside deserve no little mention as it was through them, and their deprivation, that I gained my first insight into the problems of slum housing. Lastly, but perhaps most importantly, my thanks go jointly to my parents and to my wife, Gro-Mette. Without their support, encouragement and understanding this book would not have been possible.

David A. Kirby
Lampeter
January, 1978.

Figures 1.2 and 2.1 are reproduced from *Design Bulletin 19 — Living in a Slum* with the permission of the Controller of Her Majesty's Stationery Office. Sources of other photographs are acknowledged in their captions.

INTRODUCTION

Since the First World War, housing has had the most direct and profound influence on town plans and, as Conzen (1960) observes, has contributed more to the spectacular expansion of built-up areas than has any other class of land-use. This is certainly true of the city in Western society as the wealth of literature on suburbanisation bears testimony and increasingly its importance is being recognised in the exploding cities of the Third World. Even so, despite its significance for both man and landscape, housing was, until recently, a subject in which relatively few geographers had taken a professional interest.

Throughout the 1960s, human geography was concerned almost exclusively with the study of spatial relationships and with the efficiency of spatial organisation. Since then a new, radical geography has emerged based on the concepts of social significance and social justice. To some, this revolution of social responsibility is 'neither new nor revolutionary' (Dickenson and Clarke, 1972, p. 25), but there can be little doubt that the 1970s have brought a change in emphasis from efficiency to equity solutions and 'a greater professional involvement with matters of contemporary concern' (Smith, 1971, p. 154).

While the foci for this new human geography have been the patterns arising from the distribution of scarce resources, several geographers have emphasised the importance of examining the relationships between social processes and spatial form. As Harvey (1973, p. 36) has suggested 'without an adequate understanding of social processes . . . we cannot hope to understand social space in all its complexity.' Increasingly, therefore, attention is being paid to the causes of social and environmental problems and the ways in which these various problems can be resolved. Such an approach inevitably necessitates analyses of policy and requires assessments of 'the assumptions of policy as well as policy itself' (Eyles, 1974, p. 65).

Although this book has not been written solely for geographers, it has been conceived within the framework of these recent developments in geography and in the belief that traditional human geography has overemphasised the study of spatial relationships and paid inadequate attention to the study of process. The aim of the book is, therefore, to examine the nature of residential obsolescence, the processes that produce its occurrence and the socio-economic consequences of renewal programmes in an attempt to determine those factors which have to be considered in policy formulation. This book is divided into two parts. Section 1 takes the form of a critical review of the major empirical and theoretical research into slum housing and residential renewal, while Section 2 is a case study of residential renewal in urban Britain.

Section 1 introduces the major theories and published research findings in the

English language concerned with the problems of unfit housing and the methods of residential renewal. In this section, attention is focused on the conflicting attitudes towards housing renewal. Originally housing was seen as a scarce resource and the duty of government to protect the less privileged members of society by ensuring that all households are accommodated in dwellings of a satisfactory standard. As the concepts of conservation of scarce resources and economic planning have gained in strength, so it would appear that the original social and philanthropic aspects of government have been tempered with economic reasoning and it has been appreciated that a nation's stock of houses represents one of its most important assets; assets which must be properly maintained and must not be allowed to fall into decay. In Britain, such examples of Government thinking are evident in the Torrens Act of 1868 (the Artisans and Labourers Dwellings Act) which empowered local authorities to close insanitary houses and in the Dennington Committee report of 1966 (*Our Older Homes: a Call for Action*) which tried to define the standard for a satisfactory house and to determine procedures for dealing with obsolete homes. Against these traditional renewal policies of clearance and new building, there has developed the view that substandard property can be utilised by, or for, those households unwilling or unable to pay for more modern accommodation. The validity of this argument is explored in Chapter 1 which examines the literature on the nature and role of the slum. This chapter (1) considers the question of what constitutes a slum and leads to a discussion, in Chapter 2, of minimum fitness standards and the problems surrounding their implementation. Chapter 3 outlines the process by which dwellings become obsolete or substandard and tries to determine what causes dwellings to become unsuitable for continued habitation. Attention here is focused on the roles of technological and social innovation and on those factors which affect the standard of accommodation perceived to be provided by both the dwelling and the residential environment. Having attempted to consider the factors which influence society's appraisal of housing standards, the following three chapters examine the methods by which the standard of accommodation can be maintained or improved. Chapter 4 considers the theoretical workings of the filtering concept and attempts to assess its practical effectiveness through an examination of published research findings. The sociological implications of slum clearance and rebuilding are considered in Chapter 5. Attention here is focused on the problems that arise when households move out of a familiar locality into, what is for them, an alien environment, frequently lacking the services and amenities essential for community development. In Chapter 6 the rehabilitation/rebuilding controversy is examined. The first part of the chapter attempts to evaluate the sociological advantages of rehabilitation over rebuilding, while the latter part concentrates on the economics of these two major forms of renewal.

As mentioned earlier, Section 2 takes the form of a case study of residential renewal in Britain. The intention is that the study will provide an empirical example of certain factors and theories under review in Section 1 and will provide the reader with an insight into the difficulties involved in resolving the slum problem. The study, based on an analysis of official published statistics and such documentary evidence as the relevant housing acts, examines the factors influencing policy formulation, the changes in policy over time and the effectiveness of the various renewal programmes. Accordingly, Chapter 7 outlines the slum problem in Britain, focusing on the origins, and the scale and spatial concentration of slum properties. Cross-sectional studies are made through time to show variations in the scale of the problem and to illustrate the way in which the definition and implementation of standards varies over time and space. The policies of successive British Governments are examined in Chapter 8 and the intention here is to emphasise the move away from dwelling renewal to area renewal and the change in emphasis from slum clearance to rehabilitation. Finally, the effectiveness of these policies is examined in Chapter 9 which takes the form of an analysis of the response of local authorities, individuals and private organisations to the various mechanisms introduced by the successive British Governments in an attempt to resolve the problems of slum properties.

Unlike many modern, socially-orientated geographical treatises, the study is apolitical. Perhaps it can be argued that this is an inherent weakness – if the author has any political bias, this should be made apparent at the outset. Throughout the analysis, however, a deliberate attempt has been made, in accordance with the traditions of academic investigation, to eliminate political and personal bias. Accordingly, the work should be seen as an attempt to provide an objective appraisal of both the problems of slum housing and the various methods used to eliminate slum housing conditions and raise the standard of residential accommodation.

While the case study is an attempt to take the reader beyond the level of theory, no attempt has been made to consider the everyday procedural problems involved in administering renewal programmes in Britain. For instance, there is no discussion of the powers and obligations of local authorities, of the various procedures for making demolition or closing orders, of the methods for dealing with clearance areas or of the calculation of compensation, etc. It is felt that these, and other issues concerned with the practical aspects of residential renewal in Britain, are adequately covered elsewhere, for example in Macey and Baker (1973) *Housing Management*. First written in 1965, but extensively revised and updated in 1973, this book outlines the powers and duties of British housing authorities and describes, from first-hand experience, the practical considerations involved in the various aspects of housing management in Britain.

SECTION 1
REVIEW OF THEORETICAL
AND EMPIRICAL RESEARCH

This section introduces the major theories and published research findings related to the problems of unfit housing and the methods of residential renewal. It examines the nature and causes of slums and slum housing and considers the problems surrounding the implementation of the three policies (filtering, slum-clearance and rehabilitation) traditionally employed to eradicate slums and raise the general standard of housing.

CHAPTER 1
SLUMS AND THE PROBLEMS OF SLUM HOUSING

Despite increasing affluence, urban renewal programmes and rapid suburbanisation, slums remain a characteristic of the major cities of most Western societies. According to Burgess's concentric zone model of city structure (Park *et al*., 1925) slums are found in the 'zone in transition' – the area immediately surrounding the city centre. Traditionally 'this is a zone of residential deterioration that used to be quite wealthy but became filled with low-income families and individuals. As a consequence, it contains the slums and rooming houses that are so common to the peripheral areas of the C.B.D.' (Yeates and Garner, 1971, p. 244.) Other writers have suggested, however, that 'while slums are primarily located in transitional areas near the C.B.D., there are pockets of them located elsewhere in the metropolitan complex, such as in older suburban areas: and an occasional "rural-fringe" slum is known to exist'. (Butler, 1976, p. 359.) Certainly areas of deteriorated housing exist outside the inner areas of most large urban conglomerations but whether these properties can be regarded as slums depends to a very large extent upon how the term 'slum' is defined. To some, slums are concentrations of housing which, through the passage of time, have fallen into a state of disrepair and no longer provide the standard of accommodation necessary for occupation. To others, slums are areas of low-cost housing in which reside the poor and the stranger. For the majority, however, the term 'slum' is less precise and often is interchanged freely with such euphemistic terms as 'twilight zone', 'low income area', 'deteriorated neighbourhood', etc. Accordingly, opinions about the permanence of slums vary considerably. To some they are an inevitable aspect of the urban scene, to others they are a desirable feature, while to yet others they are a feature which can and must, be eliminated as rapidly as possible. Before any conclusion can be reached about the nature and permanence of the slum problem, therefore, it is necessary to examine the nature, role and causes of slums and slum properties.

THE NATURE OF SLUMS

There is no precise dictionary definition of the term 'slum' which, as the writers of the *Encyclopaedia of Urban Planning* (Whittick, 1974, p. 905) observe, 'is of comparatively modern origin (1912), possibly a contraction of "slump", meaning to fall or sink. . .' If this is correct, it may be inferred that the term 'slum' refers to a decline or deterioration in standards. In the context of urban society, it would seem to be related to a decline in the standard or quality of the environment, both physical and social, in which people live.

Several definitions of 'slum' exist and a cursory examination reveals a distinct dichotomy between the physical and social aspects of slums. Many definitions, particularly those forming the basis for governmental action, emphasise the physical environment, possibly because it is easier to monitor and identify physical, rather than human deterioration. In Britain, for instance, a slum was defined, under Section 1 of the 1930 Housing Act, as an area in which 'the narrowness, closeness and bad arrangement, or the bad condition of streets and houses or groups of houses within such an area, or the want of light, air, ventilation and proper conveniences and other sanitary defects, or one or more of such causes as are dangerous or injurious to the health of the inhabitants of the building'. While being clearer and a little more concise, the American legislation of the same period placed similar emphasis on the physical characteristics of the building and its environment. In Sections 2 and 3 of the Housing Act of 1937, a slum was defined as 'any area where dwellings predominate which, by reason of dilapidation, overcrowding, faulty arrangement or design, lack of ventilation, light or sanitation facilities, or any combination of these factors, are detrimental to safety, health or morals'. However, not all of the definitions emphasising the physical characteristics of slums stem from Government legislation. In his book, *Slums and Housing: History, Conditions, Policy*, James Ford (1936, p. 11) suggests that a slum is 'a residential area in which the housing is so deteriorated, so substandard or so unwholesome as to be a menace to the health, safety, morality or welfare of the occupants'.

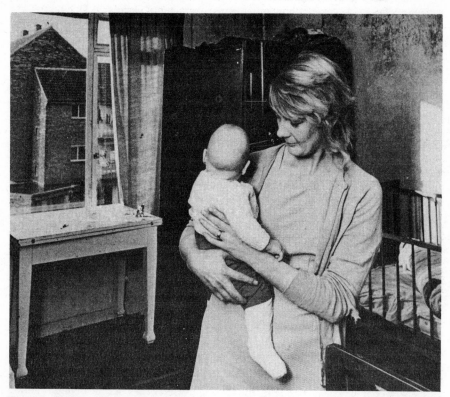

Fig. 1.1 The housing is so deteriorated, so substandard or so unwholesome as to be a menace to the health, safety, morality or welfare of the occupants (SHELTER picture library).

Each of these definitions raises a number of interesting points. While emphasising the physical characteristics of buildings and areas, it is clear that concern is for the welfare of the inhabitants; it is appreciated that the problems of the slum are not simply those of poor houses. However, a somewhat deterministic philosophy underlies each of the definitions; each definition seems to imply a causal relationship between poor physical conditions and social problems. If this is the case, it is conceivable that the eradication of poor quality housing will resolve the social problems which attend these environmental conditions. Second, while specifying the conditions which can cause an area to be regarded as a slum, each of the three definitions is highly subjective; there is no specification of what constitutes 'faulty arrangement', for instance, or of what can be considered as inadequate ventilation, lighting or sanitation. Indeed, the criteria for determining slums are, like the criteria for identifying individual houses unfit for continued occupation, both subjective and relative; what is regarded as a slum in one area need not be similarly regarded in another.

Increasingly, it is becoming apparent that a slum is something more than dilapidated housing and more recent definitions have paid considerably more attention to the sociological characteristics. A typical definition might be 'a genuine social community in the culture of poverty with all of the institutions of support and adjustment and accommodation new urban migrants as well as low income groups need.' (Wingo, 1966, p. 145.) While this, and similar definitions, emphasise the sociological aspects of the slum, they fail to convey anything of the social character of slum areas – to portray the vibrant subculture of the slum so vividly conveyed in *Street Corner Society* (Foote Whyte, 1943). Clearly slums differ but 'we think of the slum as the abode of half-starved, filthily-clothed children, of diseased and crippled individuals; a place of poverty, wretchedness, ignorance and vice.' (Conference on Home Building and Home

Fig. 1.2 The abode of half-starved, filthily-clothed children, of disease and crippled individuals: a place of poverty, wretchedness and ignorance.

Ownership, 1931.) All too frequently, moreover, it is, as Foote Whyte (1943, p. 15) describes, 'the home of racketeers and corrupt politicians, of poverty and crime, of subversive beliefs and activities'.

Several studies have noted this close correlation between slum areas and the distribution within the city of ill health, mental illness (Castle and Gittus, 1957; Dunham, 1937; Mintz and Schwarz, 1964; Timms, 1965), vice (Reckless, 1926) and delinquency and crime (Castle and Gittus, 1957; Schmid, 1960; Shaw and McKay, 1942). However, these essentially ecological studies do not claim a causal relationship between such social characteristics and poor housing. Certainly a direct relationship is known to exist between insanitary conditions and certain physical illnesses (Clarke, 1926; Robertson, 1919) and, as the following quotation suggests, it can be argued that harsh environmental conditions might be responsible for certain psychological disorders and, perhaps, for certain forms of deviant behaviour.

Across the hall from this family lives Leslie and his family of six. This room was in no better condition than the next in this house, or indeed most of this area: the wallpaper is stained, patchy and peeling. The room being old and lofty is difficult to keep warm and like all the places that we visited had an all pervading smell of leaking gas and stale urine. Leslie himself had just been released from the Psychiatric Ward of Glasgow Infirmary. He suffered from recurrent fits as a result of drug addiction and had spent time in hospital for a cure. His comments revealed a sensitive man unable to cope with the misery of living idle in such squalor. He reasoned that alcoholism and drug addiction begin as an attempt to escape from the pain of living in the Gorbals. (Watney, Waymouth and Bradshaw, 1965, p. 3.)

While this may be true, it can be counter argued that, by nature, the slum dweller is inadequate and unable to cope with such environmental conditions. If this is the case, perhaps in attempting to explain this and other such relationships, attention should be focused on the characteristics of slum dwellers and an attempt should be made to understand why they live in such areas.

THE CHARACTERISTICS OF SLUM DWELLERS

In their book, *The Cost of Slums in Newark,* Rumney and Shuman (1946) suggest that the vicious and criminal drift into the slum where they are able to carry on their activities 'because they are lost from view in the strangeness and social confusion of the area'. While not everyone would agree that the slum lacks social order (Suttles, 1968), it is generally accepted that it is, for many, a place in which to hide. Not all slum dwellers are, however, refugees from the law. Many are what Rumney and Shuman call families 'with a normal physical and mental inheritance' who are 'marooned in the slum by misfortune'. Ultimately these families absorb into their own lives the 'bizarre habits and disorders of the transitional society' and drift along in 'a state of chronic failure'.

This suggests two types of slum dweller – those who desire to live in the area in an attempt to achieve obscurity and those who, as a result of misfortune and, possibly, personal inadequacy, find themselves trapped in the area. The concept of involuntary residence and inadequacy is further emphasised by Stokes (1962). In this paper, which deals essentially with the Third world cities, Stokes (p. 188) argues that the function of the slum is 'to house those classes which do not participate directly in the economic and social life of the city'. This may not be entirely correct but the concept does permit Stokes to identify four types of slum dwellers based on their psychological attitude towards moving up the social scale and the socio-economic barriers they are likely to encounter. Initially two main groups of slum dwellers are identified – those with 'hope' who intend to better themselves and believe self-betterment is possible, and those with 'despair' who either have no desire to move up the social scale or believe that any attempt to change status will be unsuccessful. Additionally, Stokes suggests that it is possible to identify one group of slum dwellers (the 'escalators') which can be expected to better itself and another (the 'non-escalators') which, for one reason or another, is likely to be denied the possibility of upward social mobility. With this fourfold typology of slum dwellers, it is argued that the slum of 'hope' is the home of the stranger. In-migrants, suggests Stokes, are either attracted to the city by the social and economic opportunities it offers or are driven from their homes elsewhere by economic, political or social upheaval. Usually, they come to the city seeking 'improvement' and the majority are absorbed into the general employable population and are able to move up the social scale. However, not all strangers are successful. Some will lack ability and others will be debarred by skin-colour or religion. These, together with those having no desire for upward mobility, are the inhabitants of the slum of 'despair.'

Stokes's model can be criticised from several points of view: it neglects the area's original residents, it fails to mention those who come to the area from within the city and it seems to suggest a mechanism whereby all of those attracted to the city by its social and economic opportunities, gravitate to the areas of poorest housing. Even so, it does provide further insight into the nature of slum dwellers and the workings of the slum.

Possibly the most perceptive and comprehensive classification is that provided by Seeley (1959) in his paper 'The slum: its nature, use and users'. Seeley's observations appear to be based on a more accurate interpretation of the role of the slum than are those of Stokes. He suggests that slums are not just dumping grounds or routes into the city but are providers of goods and services, many of which are demanded by the city's non-slum population. For many of the residents of such an area a slum is 'a set of opportunities for behaviour which they want . . . to indulge in or to be permitted' (Seeley, 1959, p. 10) and, for others, it is 'a set of necessities to which, despite their wants, they have been reduced' (op. cit., p. 10). In this respect, Seeley appears to be in broad agreement with Rumney and Shuman. However, like Stokes, Seeley recognises that change is possible and he identifies two groups – those who feel they are in a slum on a temporary basis and those who feel they are there permanently. These distinctions permit the identification of four major types of slum dweller – the 'permanent neces-sitarians', the 'temporary necessitarians', the 'permanent opportunists' and the 'tem-porary opportunists'.

The 'permanent necessitarians' – people who feel they cannot leave the area and who will or can do nothing to find alternative accommodation – include the 'indolent' who, possibly from inherited characteristics, disease, maleducation, malnutrition, con-tinuous defeat, etc. display a general apathy or immobility; the 'adjusted poor' who, although destitute or nearly destitute, so value their independence that they have accepted life in the hovels of the area because they are available at a low rent; 'social outcasts' such as alcoholics, drug addicts, drug pushers, prostitutes, pimps and others whose illegal or (at best) marginally legal activities exclude them from the better neighbourhoods. The 'temporary necessitarians' include the 'respectable poor' and the 'trapped'. Financially, the 'respectable poor' are often as destitute as the 'adjusted poor' but they have not adjusted, or are unreconciled, to life in the slum. Their values and associations are frequently outside the area in which they reside and usually their life-styles are those of a socially higher class. Normally a law-abiding group, they live in the hope that 'things will take a turn for the better' and they will be able to live more nearly where they feel they belong. The 'trapped' are people who bought or inherited a house in a slum area when it was not so run-down. Either they refuse to accept that the area is as bad as it is or they find themselves unable to realise the true value (in their terms) of their property because of the surrounding physical and social blight.

The third group, the 'permanent opportunists' are those who live in the slum because of the opportunities it affords. Seeley calls these the 'fugitives', the 'unfindables', the 'models' and the 'sporting crowd'. The 'fugitives' are either those who live a more or less permanent life of subterfuge and flight (usually from the law) or those who have decided to avoid the business or professional competition of the better areas. The former are clearly seeking the anonymity of the slum while the latter (frequently doctors, lawyers, businessmen, etc.) are either escaping from the status struggles of the outside world or are looking for a more easily attained economic niche. The 'unfindables' are not so much people in flight as people whose individualism and detachment lead them to seek no clear social identity. The 'models', states Seeley, are rare but interesting. They are people who conceive of themselves as social or religious missionaries. By comparison, the 'sporting crowd' are a range of characters noted for their appreciation of a 'good time'. They live in the slum because living in a slum leaves them money to spend on 'other things'; because having spent a large proportion of their money on 'other things', they only have enough for slum rents; because the slum provides the 'other things' they desire and because the slum is the place where they can meet people with similar interests. Associated with this group, Seeley suggests, are the 'roughnecks' – those who make it unsafe for others to be in the area. The fourth major group which can be identified is the 'temporary opportunists'. According to Seeley this group is not only important numerically but also because the slum is a way to self-improvement and independence for its members. Within this group, three sub-types can be identified. These are the 'beginners', the 'climbers' and the 'entrepreneurs'. The 'beginners' are mostly the immigrants to the city for whom the slum is simply their first area of settlement. Many of these are young married couples with slim financial, educational and psychological resources. The 'climbers' are similar but often they have lived in the area for some time in a state of self-denial and self-sacrifice, trying to accumulate enough goods, money and 'know how' to move to a better area. For many, the time to move is always a little later. Seeley's last group is the 'entrepreneurs' – those who establish a small business in the slum or, more frequently, live off the slum itself. Often they purchase property and usually they eventually move to a better neighbourhood on the profits of the various slum properties they own.

Perhaps it can be argued that some of Seeley's conditions are now somewhat dated. For instance, changed Government attitudes and increasing permissiveness has made vice almost a respectable occupation in many societies; certainly one that is no longer confined to the shadowy streets of the city slums. Even so, the sort of people Seeley identifies are readily recognisable in the slums of contemporary society: they are as much in evidence in Liverpool Seven as they are on the streets of Harlem.

ATTITUDES OF SLUM DWELLERS TO MOVING

To the majority of non-slum dwellers, living conditions in a slum might appear to be so undesirable that they would not expect any of the residents to want to remain in the area. If the various classifications of slum dwellers are correct, however, it would seem that, in terms of their attitudes towards the area, slum dwellers might be divided into two groups – those who want or intend to move to another area and those who have chosen to live in the area and might be expected to remain. Thus it might be anticipated that any survey of residents' attitudes would, if the classifications are correct, yield a large proportion of responses indicating a positive identification with the area and a desire to remain, despite the physical condition of the property.

Results of a survey in the St Mary's Ward of Oldham, a typical nineteenth-century industrial town in Lancashire (England), would seem to suggest that many slum residents have an extremely strong attachment to their locality. In 1962, when the survey was undertaken, the area contained 981 houses of which no more than 3 per cent had been passed by the Medical Officer of Health as being fit for human habitation. Only 7 per cent were unoccupied, however, and the remainder housed some 2 370 people in 946 separate households at a gross density of 66 persons per acre. The results of the survey, outlined in the Ministry of Housing and Local Government (1970a) publication *Living in a Slum: a Study of St. Mary's Oldham,* produced no evidence to suggest that St Mary's was a transient area as Stokes's theories imply. Some transients were identified and these were found to be indigenous young couples living in the area until they could obtain better accommodation elsewhere. Generally, residential mobility levels were found to be extremely low. Over half (59 per cent) of the 132 respondents had either spent all of their lives in the area or had lived there for over twenty years. It must be appreciated, however, that Oldham is no longer a major centre of industrial activity. Indeed, recent years have witnessed considerable out-migration and in this respect, perhaps, the town contrasts markedly with many of the major cities of Europe, America and, particularly, the Third World where Stokes formulated his ideas.

The survey revealed that only about 17 per cent of the respondents wanted to move from the area. Of these, about one-third said they would like 'somewhere more open', 'not so built up' or 'somewhere healthier and cleaner', etc. while another third wanted to move because they thought St Mary's was dirty or the neighbours were 'rough'. The remaining 33 per cent wanted to be nearer work, their friends or their relatives. The results seem to suggest, therefore, that only about 11 per cent of the respondents wanted to move to a better district in an attempt to escape the squalid physical environment.

Approximately 7 per cent were unconcerned whether they moved or stayed but the majority (76 per cent) wanted to remain in the area. Two main reasons were given for not wanting to move. Slightly more than 25 per cent wanted to stay because they felt socially dependent upon the area, while a further 25 per cent stressed the area's convenience. For the remainder, both reasons were of equal importance.

The results of the study would seem to support Seeley's observations that many of the residents of a slum live there by choice and wish to remain in the area. However, it should be appreciated that the survey was measuring the respondent's attitude towards staying in the area after redevelopment and not the respondent's attitude towards the slum as it was. By comparison, a study of slum clearance areas in Leeds (Wilkinson and Sigsworth, 1963) revealed that 82 per cent of the inhabitants wanted to move. Here the respondents were asked whether they really wanted to move and it is not clear whether the question relates to a change of house, a change of area or both.

Further support for Seeley's observations comes from America where Fried and Gleicher (1961) examined the pre-relocation attitudes of residents in the West End of Boston. In spite of the very considerable differences, particularly in scale, between Boston and Oldham, Fried and Gleicher's results are very similar to those generated by the survey of St Mary's Ward. Indeed, Fried and Gleicher come to the conclusion that they 'cannot readily accept those impressions of a slum which suggest a highly transient population' (op. cit., p. 306). Some 55 per cent of their sample had lived in the study area for over twenty years and almost one-quarter had been born there. What is more, their findings indicated that some three-quarters of the sample liked the area while approximately 71 per cent regarded it as their real home. In studying the reasons for satisfaction, Fried and Gleicher found that although rents in the area were low, they were rarely mentioned when discussing satisfactory aspects of either the area or the accommodation. For the majority, the two most important components were found to be the vast set of social networks that characterise such localities and the sense of belonging generated within the area through its common experience and usage by the residents.

It would appear, therefore, that within any slum population, there is a large proportion of residents who regard the area as home and are consequently reluctant to move. Clearly it can be argued that the findings of these studies are somewhat suspect since they were conducted in pre-relocation situations when sentiment and concern about the future and the unknown might be expected to produce particularly high levels of area loyalty. However, there is a wealth of literature on established working-class neighbourhoods in inner city areas (Mogey, 1956; Kerr, 1958) which demonstrates the strength of attachment that can be generated in such an area. For instance, in *Family and Kinship in East London,* Young and Willmott (1962) quote numerous residents who summarise most vividly the sense of belonging in the Bethnal Green area of London. As one resident eloquently observed 'I was bred and born in Bethnal Green and my parents and their parents before them: no, I wouldn't leave Bethnal Green, I wouldn't take a threepenny bus ride outside Bethnal Green.' (Op. cit., p. 113.) Perhaps such sentiments might be thought to be extreme until it is realised that there are numerous stories of Bethnal Green families who, during the Second World War, 'would rather camp in the kitchens of their uninhabitable blitzed houses or sleep in public shelters than accept accommodation in another area of the borough' (Glass and Frenkel, 1946, p. 43).

As Fried and Gleicher (1961) observe, it is extremely difficult for the educated, highly mobile middle classes to see the importance of the area as a home to the residents of a slum and for them to appreciate the significance of local people and local places. However, it is this basic sense of identity which comes from living in a particular locality that provides the basis for the extensive levels of social integration which are so frequently characteristic of slum (and other working-class) areas.

CONCLUSION: THE PROBLEMS OF SLUMS

There is no question that the slum areas of cities are, no matter how they are defined, perceived as a problem. Yet to what extent is it necessary to regard the slum as a problem if, as it would seem, the majority of slum dwellers chose to live in such areas and are content to remain there?

In the first place, it must be appreciated that a problem is primarily a state of mind – it is a situation that worries members of society either as individuals or groups. Thus a problem only exists when it is perceived. Second, a problem may be perceived differently by different individuals and different sectors of society. For instance, opposition to a proposed programme of inter-urban highway development might come from those concerned about the ensuing loss of revenue to rail and competing forms of transportation, from those concerned about the country's inevitably increasing dependence on oil as an energy source, from those concerned about increasing pollution levels and from those concerned about the preservation and conservation of the environment. Each group perceives the problem as the impact of the highway proposals but the perceived effects are different for each.

In his paper 'Government and slum housing: some general considerations', Friedman (1967) suggests that in most countries the slum is perceived as a problem by at least three groups of people – those, possibly a minority, who live in the slum itself; those who live in non-slum areas and, usually, the local and national governments. Each of these

Fig. 1.3 It is the basic sense of identity that comes from living in a particular locality that provides the basis for the extensive levels of social integration so frequently characteristic of slum areas (SHELTER picture library).

groups perceives the slum problem differently. For those slum dwellers who see the slum as a problem, perhaps their concern is focused on the deficiencies in their own living standards and on the discomfort, stigma and pain associated with life in a slum. Non-slum dwellers cannot perceive the slum in this way since, by definition, their experience of a slum is restricted to that of an outside observer. No matter how long an outsider voluntarily spends in a slum, he cannot view it in the same way as a slum dweller, primarily because his roots are not in the slum and he knows he can 'escape'. For many of this group the slum is a threat both to them as individuals and to the society to which they belong. These people might see the slum as a breeding ground for crime, violence, disease and other anti-social disorders. Their concern is focused largely on the effect of the slum on the safety of non-slum dwellers as individuals, but also on its impact on the external image of the society of which they are a part. Other non-slum dwellers have a more altruistic, less self-centred approach. For this group, conscience and conviction, rather than self-interest, are the predominant motivations and the problem of the slum is perceived as that of 'bettering' the living conditions, life-styles or values of the slum dweller. According to Friedman, Government reacts to, rather than initiates interest. If this is the case, the Government's perception of the slum problem is a reaction to the problem as perceived by the electorate. Perhaps this view of the derived interest of Government is something of an oversimplification but Friedman's attempt to identify interests in the slum problem does provide an insight into the various ways in which the problem can be perceived.

Not only is the slum problem perceived in different ways by various groups but it manifests itself in a variety of forms and it is possible for people with the same attitudes to emphasise different aspects of the problem. For instance, certain social reformers may concern themselves with trying to eliminate drug addiction or alcoholism while others may focus their attention on improving housing and sanitary conditions. In his book *The Slums: Challenge and Response,* Hunter (1968) identifies several separate but connected elements which go to make up the slum problem: these, he suggests, are poverty, run-down housing, crowding, concentration of lower-class people, racial concentration, concentration of low educational achievement, low skill and cultural limitations, many welfare cases, internal mobility, crime, health problems, broken families, relocation problems, inadequate community services, skid row, isolation and alienation, dirt, fire hazards, language problems and the slum atmosphere. While the list can be criticised from several viewpoints, it does give some indication of the extensive set of conditions which constitute the problems of the slum. Furthermore, Hunter recognises that many of the elements are interconnected and it is not possible to deal with each in isolation. As Jane Jacobs (1964, p. 284) observes 'slums and their populations are the victims (and perpetuators) of seemingly endless troubles that reinforce each other.' They are, in fact, vicious circles in which cause and effect become confused simply because the elements of the system link and relink with each other in such complicated ways. The solution, as Jacobs points out, is to identify the key link. In the past, the key to the problem of slums has been perceived as the problem of slum housing – eradicate slum housing and the slum problem is resolved. As subsequent chapters will demonstrate, this is not the case. Even so, the existence of slum housing remains one of the most serious problems facing contemporary society.

CHAPTER 2
OBSOLETE HOUSING AND
THE PROBLEM OF UNFITNESS

The problem of slum housing is the problem of obsolete dwellings: dwellings which society deems to be unsatisfactory for continued occupation. In contemporary society the problem might be regarded as one of ideological creation, reflecting the belief that the individual has the right to certain minimum housing conditions. Accordingly, it is a problem shrouded in controversy since the extent to which society (in the form of Government) has the right to dictate to its subjects the conditions under which it is 'fit' for them to live is a point of philosophical and political debate. Historically, however, the principle behind the introduction of standards of minimum fitness was the protection of society; controls were introduced originally to guard against fire and maintain public health and morals. With improved living conditions in the developed countries of the world, so there has been a change in the nature of the controls. As Hole (1965, p. 142) has observed 'now that public health has improved and overcrowding has been virtually eliminated, the earlier emphasis in housing standards on health and morals has been submerged; criteria for modern standards are convenience and amenity.' Clearly this is something of an overstatement even in the developed countries of the world but it emphasises the flexible nature of standards and raises the question of whether standards should be raised to meet social objectives. For many, this is a question that merits serious discussion 'not least because of the economic costs that would be involved, both for government and individual households' (Watson, 1974, p. 61). For instance, if standards were set too high, many dwellings would become obsolete long before the end of their expected life (usually at least sixty years), while the housing built to the new standards would be too costly for many households, particularly those in greatest need.

Clearly, considerable controversy accompanies the implementation of minimum fitness standards for housing in the developed countries of the world. In Third World countries, however, such controversy is, perhaps, less noticeable since the housing problems of many Third World cities are more akin to those of nineteenth-century England, than twentieth-century Western society. Accordingly, housing standards in the Third World are often concerned as much with the protection of society and the improvement of general living conditions as they are with the rights of the individual. This is an important point since it demonstrates that standards are not absolute – they are, in fact, related to the living standards of the society in which they operate. As a consequence, there is no uniform or international definition of unfitness. Despite its close involvement in the question of international comparison, the United Nations recognises this and points out that, 'with respect to the detailed aspects of housing, meaningful standards can be developed only at the national or local levels. It is left to the countries themselves to establish and define the standards used to differentiate between "acceptable living quarters" and "unacceptable living quarters".' (United Nations, 1967, p. 11.)

This question of minimum fitness is complicated still further by individual preference. As Duncan (1971, p. xi) observes 'some families have no need for a garden while others enjoy tending a fair-sized area. Some wish to live close to a town centre for the convenience this brings; others . . . do not mind a journey to work if they can live in more open surroundings.' Clearly, different people have different concepts of the desirable characteristics of a house. Even so, despite the immense variety of conditions and preferences and the accompanying philosophical/political debate, minimum fitness standards do exist and it is through the implementation of these standards that the problem of slum housing is made manifest.

MINIMUM FITNESS STANDARDS IN ENGLAND AND WALES

The definition of individual unfit housing operating in England and Wales in 1977 is based on the 1946 recommendations of the Miles Mitchell Sub-Committee on Standards of Fitness for Habitation. These recommendations were embodied in Section 4(1) of the Housing Act, 1957. The Act states that 'in determining . . . whether a house is unfit for human habitation, regard shall be had to its condition in respect of the following matters, that is to say:

(a) repair
(b) stability
(c) freedom from damp
(d) natural lighting
(e) ventilation
(f) water supply
(g) drainage and sanitary conveniences
(h) facilities for storage, preparation and cooking of food and for the disposal of waste water.

and the house shall be deemed to be unfit for human habitation if and only if it is so far defective in one or more of the said matters that it is not reasonably suited for occupation in that condition.' (Housing Act, 1957.) This, then, is the basis of the statutory definition of unfit housing. It has remained virtually unchanged since its inception in 1957 although in February 1965 the Central Housing Advisory Sub-Committee on Standards of Housing Fitness was appointed to consider and make recommendations on 'the practicability of specifying objective criteria for the purposes of slum clearance, rectification of disrepair and other housing powers relating to minimum tolerable standards of housing accommodation'. The Committee came to the conclusion that the 1957 standards provided a good foundation on which to build and, in the report of its findings (Central Housing Advisory Committee, 1966), recommended that the new standard for a satisfactory dwelling should be:

(a) that the environmental conditions must be satisfactory and that the dwelling should:
(b) be in a stable condition, in good state of repair and free from damp;
(c) be satisfactorily arranged internally;
(d) have adequate natural lighting to each habitable room and working kitchen;
(e) have adequate points for artificial lighting by gas or electricity in each room, staircase, passage and cellar in use;

(f) be provided with adequate means of ventilation throughout;

(g) have a suitably located and satisfactory internal w.c. for the exclusive use of the occupants;

(h) have a fixed bath or shower in an adequately ventilated compartment, separate from any habitable room or kitchen;

(i) have a suitably located wash-hand basin;

(j) have an adequate and wholesome supply of water for all domestic purposes with both hot and cold water provided to sink, wash-hand basin and bath or shower;

(k) have a satisfactory system for the drainage and disposal of foul and surface water;

(l) have a suitable sink and impervious draining surface, suitable and adequately ventilated provision for storage of food, and either a satisfactory built-in cooker or a gas or electricity connection for a cooker: generally the disposition of these facilities should make the preparation and cooking of food capable of being carried out in a convenient and hygienic manner;

(m) have adequate provision for the heating of living rooms, bedrooms and the kitchen;

(n) have adequate points for the use of electric appliances where an electricity supply is reasonably available;

(o) have adequate space for facilities for washing and drying clothes;

(p) have proper provision for storing fuel (where required);

(q) have satisfactory provision for storing refuse;

(r) have a satisfactory access to all doors and outbuildings; and that

(s) dwellings in blocks of five or more storeys should be served by a lift where it is physically and economically practicable to provide one.

Only one of these proposals (c) was adopted. In the 1968 White Paper *Old Houses into New Homes*, the Government stated its belief that the 1957 criteria by which a dwelling is judged to be fit or unfit were still the right ones but acknowledged that 'an important contributing factor making for an unfit house may be that it has a very bad internal layout: for example, a w.c. opening directly from the living room or kitchen and narrow, steep or winding staircases' (Ministry of Housing and Local Government, 1968a, p. 9). Accordingly, the standard was amended under Section 71 of the Housing Act, 1969 to include internal arrangement and, at the same time, 'storage' was deleted from paragraph (h) of the original 1957 Act definition. In essence, therefore, the definition of unfitness has remained unchanged for the past twenty years or more.

While this definition relates to factors causing individual dwellings to be regarded as unfit for human occupation, further definitions relate to environmental conditions which cause residential areas or groups of dwellings to be so regarded. For instance, Section 5 of the 1957 Act states that, quite apart from the provisions of Section 4, any back-to-back dwellings shall be regarded as unfit for human habitation while Section 42 defines those circumstances in which *areas* of inadequate housing can be identified. Commonly referred to as the 'bad arrangement' clause, it specifies that an area must contain two or more houses which are unfit (as defined in Section 4) or houses which are, by reason of their bad arrangement, or the narrowness or bad arrangement of the streets, dangerous or injurious to the health of the area's inhabitants.

Clearly, this provision adds another dimension to the concept of unfitness. Here concern is focused on the congestion of buildings and the narrowness of streets and back-alleys. Thus it can be seen that accommodation can be regarded as being unfit for human occupation either because of the unfitness of the individual dwelling or because of the bad arrangement of dwellings in an area. It can also be seen that interpretation of the standards is highly subjective. For instance, each of the nine points listed in the amended definition of individual unfitness requires a decision on the seriousness of the defect. Similarly, the bad arrangement clause requires a matter of judgement when attempting to determine the effect of the layout of an area on the health of its inhabitants.

In some respects this subjectivity of interpretation is one of the great strengths of the legislation since it permits flexibility in the interpretation of housing policy. As will be shown later, however, the lack of standardisation frequently results in considerable differences in the way in which the standard is interpreted in different parts of the country and at different periods in time. Invariably, an authority with a daunting slum problem will assess its dwellings on the basis of what it can hope to deal with during its plan period rather than apply the more stringent interpretation that might have been applied in an area where the problem is less acute. This problem of subjectivity was recognised by the 1965 Sub-Committee on Standards of Housing Fitness. However, the

Fig. 2.1 Areas can be regarded as being unfit for habitation because they are dangerous or injurious to the health of the residents.

Committee pointed out that 'definitions must neither be too sophisticated nor too difficult to operate if they are to be useful to local authorities in day-to-day action' (Central Housing Advisory Committee 1966, p. 6) and argued that since, 'in the last resort, decisions must depend on the judgement of an experienced person' (op. cit., p. 6) there is no advantage in introducing a system that is more objective in appearance if it merely conceals the same reliance on judgement.

INDEXES OF UNFITNESS

Similar reservations about the difficulties involved in ensuring that the same criteria are applied with equal objectivity throughout the country are expressed by Duncan in his study *Measuring Housing Quality* (Duncan, 1971). Duncan criticises the statutory definition of unfitness because it gives no indication of the degree of unfitness, the nature of the defects nor any indication of the potential for renovation. Accordingly, he attempts to assess the various methods which have been devised to eliminate these deficiencies. As he recognises in his conclusions, it is not easy to summarise the wide range of indexes discussed in the report but it would seem from the vast research input into the methods of measuring housing quality that there is a need for more dependable and useful information on the state of the housing stock. While the studies have varied considerably in their origins and scope, they have all attempted to measure, as Duncan recognises, the extent to which various factors compare against a declared set of standards. Two approaches can be identified – one which allocates penalty scores on the basis of the relative seriousness of the deficiencies of a dwelling or neighbourhood to its occupants, and the other which allocates a scale of penalty points based on the cost of bringing the substandard dwelling or environment up to a specific standard. Each of the approaches has its own inherent weaknesses. With the former, the allocation of penalty points remains somewhat arbitrary. With the latter, arbitrary judgements are virtually obviated by the use of actual costs or penalty points based on costs. Even so, it is not possible to compare findings between areas, particularly over time, because of the variations that exist in building and material costs.

Perhaps the most widely used example of the former approach is the appraisal method of the American Public Health Association (Table 2.1). The method, intended for use in selected areas known to contain poor or mediocre housing, involves the assignment of penalty scores (determined by a panel of experts) to conditions that fail to meet accepted housing and environmental standards. As can be seen from the schedule, appraisal is carried out separately on dwelling facilities, maintenance, occupancy and neighbourhood environment but it is possible to derive a single index for each dwelling unit. Irrespective of the total penalty score, dwellings are classified as substandard if they have one or more basic deficiencies requiring drastic corrective action. The most impressive features of the method are 'its comprehensiveness, its comparative objectivity and the fact that results can be given a locational pattern' (Duncan, 1971, p. 26). The main objection to the method appears to be that it is too time-consuming. However, Hemdahl (1959) has observed that at least one-third of the forty-two American cities he surveyed in the early 1950s were adopting the appraisal method or an adaptation of it.

In Britain, a modified version of the appraisal method is the Housing Defects Index devised by the Scottish Housing Advisory Committee and outlined in Appendix III of its 1967 publication, *Scotland's Older Houses*. In its original form the index is not entirely satisfactory since it does not attempt to measure environmental conditions and does not permit the identification of major and minor defects. As a consequence, further modifications have been made but these revisions have not been tested. The Index of Decay is a British example of a subjectively derived index. In *Urban Decay: an Analysis and Policy*, Medhurst and Parry Lewis (1969) outline their attempts to construct an index intended to measure decay in a large Lancashire town. Observers were asked to note the presence or absence of selected dwelling and environmental attributes and penalty scores, determined by a team of experts, were allocated according to the degree of severity as shown in Table 2.2.

Although the results of the survey gave encouraging correlations with census data, the method has several inherent weaknesses. Since the study is carried out without gaining access to buildings, it only measures the external condition of property. While this enables the exercise to be conducted in a relatively short period of time, little is

Table 2.1 Schedule of American Public Health Association Appraisal items and maximum standard penalty (after Duncan)

DWELLING CONDITIONS

Item	Maximum score	Penalty
A. Facilities		
1. *Structure*: main access	6	
2. Water supply (source for structure)	25	
3. Sewer connection	25	
4. Daylight obstruction	20	
5. Stairs and fire escapes	30	
6. Public hall lighting	18	
7. *Unit*: location in structure	8	
8. Kitchen facilities	24	
9. Toilet*	45	
10. Bath*	20	
11. Water supply (location and type for unit)	15	
12. Washing facilities	8	
13. Dual egress	30	
14. Electric lighting	15	
15. Central heating	3	
16. Rooms lacking installed heater	20	
17. Rooms lacking windows	30	
18. Rooms lacking closet	8	
19. Rooms of substandard area	10	
20. Combined room facilities‡	—	360
B. Maintenance		
21. Toilet condition index	12	
22. Deterioration index§	50	
23. Infestation index§	15	
24. Sanitary index§	30	
25. Basement condition index	13	120
C. Occupancy		
26. Room crowding: persons per room	30	
27. Room crowding: persons per sleeping room	25	
28. Room crowding: sleeping area per person	30	
29. Area crowding: non-sleeping area per person	25	
30. Doubling of basic facilities	10	120
Maximum dwelling score		600

to be continued

Table 2.1 *(continued)*

NEIGHBOURHOOD ENVIRONMENT

Item	Maximum score	Penalty
A. Land crowding		
1. Coverage by structures	24	
2. Residential building density	20	
3. Population density	10	
4. Residential yard areas	17	70
B. Non-residential land uses		
5. Areal incidence of non-residential uses	13	
6. Linear incidences of non-residential uses	13	
7. Specific non-residential nuisances and hazards	30	
8. Hazards to morals and the public peace	10	
9. Smoke incidence	6	72
C. Hazards and nuisances for transportation system		
10. Street traffic	20	
11. Railroads or switchyards	24	
12. Airports or airlines†	20	64
D. Hazards and nuisances from natural causes		
13. Surface flooding	20	
14. Swamps and marshes†	24	
15. Topography	16	60
E. Inadequate utilities and sanitation		
16. Sanitary sewage system	24	
17. Public water supply	20	
18. Streets and walks	10	54
F. Inadequate basic community facilities		
19. Elementary public schools	10	
20. Public playgrounds	8	
21. Public playfields	4	
22. Other public parks	8	
23. Public transportation	12	
24. Food store†	6	48
Maximum environmental total		*368*

* Item score is total of subscores for location, type and sharing of toilet or bath facilities.
† Provisional item – not tested.
‡ Item score is total of scores for items 16–19 inclusive – it is just recorded for analysis.
§ Item score is total of subscores for structures and unit.

Table 2.2 Weights used in the Index of Decay

	MUCH	SOME	LITTLE	NONE
Physical condition				
Surface deterioration	5	3	1	0
Paint peeling	3	2	1	0
Displaced roof units	9	5	1	0
Broken glazing	7	3	1	0
Gutter-/down-pipe leaking	7	3	1	0
Settlement evident	11	6	3	0
Timber rot	8	4	2	0
Sagging roof	10	6	2	0
Environmental condition				
Offensive smells	3	2	1	0
Air pollution	3	2	1	0
Noise	3	2	1	0
Grass or trees	0	1	2	3
Litter	3	2	1	0
Parked vehicles	3	2	1	0

known about the degree of correlation between internal and external conditions and assumptions about the standard of fitness for occupation could be misleading if based solely on external appearance. Another area of weakness surrounds the assessment of the levels of severity. As the authors point out, 'there may be observer prejudice, either because of different observers or because the same observer may vary his standards from day-to-day or from one type of housing to another.' (op. cit., p. 120.) With observer training and checking procedures, this problem can be overcome.

A much more fundamental weakness is the fact that, for certain items, there are obvious difficulties in obtaining a reliable assessment. For instance, the intensity of 'offensive smells' or 'parked vehicles' may vary over time, while it may be difficult to determine the severity of a leaking gutter or downpipe under certain weather conditions. Even so, the technique provides a simple and relatively quick method of identifying urban decay.

Duncan outlines three indexes based on estimates of the cost of bringing defective dwelling units up to a given standard. However, details of two, the House Condition Index and the Scottish Development Department's Indices of Repair Costs, are not widely available. The House Condition Index was used to assess housing conditions in the Deeplish area of Rochdale, Lancashire, and is described, somewhat inadequately perhaps, in the 1966 Ministry of Housing and Local Government publication *The Deeplish Study: Improvement Possibilities in a District of Rochdale*. After being used in this study, it was generally recognised that further work would be required before the usefulness of the technique could be assessed. The indices of Repair Costs were developed in 1968 by the Housing Division of the Scottish Development Department and are outlined in an unpublished report entitled *Tenements in Rutherglen: a Report on the Housing Condition Survey*. In his appraisal of the technique, Duncan suggests that its scope is extremely limited since it was only devised to study a compact tenement area and it might be difficult to obtain comparable results for a different area. A similar criticism can be levelled at the third of the economic appraisal indexes, the Survey of

Table 2.3 Survey of Housing and Environmental Deficiency Index (after Duncan)

PENALTY POINTS FOR DEFICIENCIES IN THE DWELLING

	Penalty points	Maximum
Condition		
Maintenance and structure good	0	
Maintenance poor, structure good	5	
Maintenance and structure poor	12	12
Basic facilities		
No fixed bath	5	
No hot water system	5	
No internal w.c.	5	15
*Type		
Detached	0	
Semi-detached	0	
Terrace	1	1
*House access		
Two entrance doors	0	
One entrance door	3	3
Outdoor private space		
Front and back garden or yard	0	
Back garden or yard only	3	
Front garden or yard only	3	
No back or front garden or yard	8	8
*Parking/garaging		
More than 1 car space per d.u.	0	
1 car space per d.u.	1	
Less than 1 car space per d.u.	5	5
Maximum penalty points for dwelling		44

PENALTY POINTS FOR DEFICIENCIES IN THE ENVIRONMENT

	Penalty points	Maximum
*Privacy		
No overlooking on either side	0	
Overlooking on one side	2	
Overlooking on both sides	5	5
Noise		
Normal residential standard	0	
Above residential but not ind./comm. std.	2	
Ind./comm. e.g. main street standard	5	5

to be continued

Table 2.3 (continued)

PENALTY POINTS FOR DEFICIENCIES IN THE ENVIRONMENT

	Penalty points	Maximum
Traffic		
Normal residential traffic	0	
Above normal residential traffic	3	
Large amount of ind. and through traffic	6	6
*Visual quality		
Higher standard than environment	0	
Same standard as environment	1	
Lower standard than environment	3	3
Access to POS		
Park/POS within 5 mins. walk	0	
No park/POS within 5 mins. walk	3	3
Access to shops and primary schools		
Primary school and shops within 5 mins. walk	0	
Primary school but no shops in 5 mins. walk	2	
Shops but no primary school in 5 mins. walk	5	
No primary school or shops in 5 mins. walk	7	7
Access to public transportation to major centre		
Less than 3 mins. walk	0	
More than 3 mins. walk	3	3
*Density		
Less than 10 d.u.'s per acre	0	
10–19 d.u.'s per acre	1	
20–29 d.u.'s per acre	3	
30 d.u.'s or more per acre	7	7
*Air pollution		
Negligible	0	
Light	3	
Heavy	9	9
*Age		
Post-war	0	
1918–1939	1	
1895–1914	2	
Pre-1895	3	3
Landscape quality		
Mature, good quality abundant landscape	0	
Immature, insufficient amounts	2	
Total or almost total lack of landscape	5	5
Maximum penalty points		56
Maximum penalty points for dwelling and environment		100

* Items which are not remediable by rehabilitation.

Housing and Environmental Deficiency. Developed for a study of housing conditions on Teesside, the technique is outlined in Volume II of the *Teesside Survey and Plan* by Wilson and Womersley (1969) and is 'one of the most penetrating of the recent attempts to measure the quality of housing and residential areas' (Duncan, 1971, p. 58). As can be seen from Table 2.3 the technique is similar to the American Public Health Authority appraisal method in that penalty points are allocated for deficiencies in the dwelling and the environment. However, each penalty point is estimated to be equivalent to a rehabilitation cost of £39 since analysis of several case studies revealed that when expressed as a unit cost per penalty point, rehabilitation costs were relatively constant at around this level.

CONCLUSION

Each of the indexes is attempting to identify a point where the severity of one condition, or several conditions in combination, makes the dwelling unsuitable for continued occupation. For instance, it has been suggested that a satisfactory house, under the revised Housing Defects Index, is one with a penalty score of 10 points or less, while a 'tolerable' dwelling has a score of between 10 and 30 deficiency points. Any dwelling with a score in excess of 30 is unsuitable for continued occupation. None of the indexes has proved to be entirely successful, however, and no universally acceptable index exists. This is partly a reflection of the extreme complexity of the conditions that prevail, but it is also a reflection of the relatively recent nature of the subject. If it is possible to identify, objectively, the point where a dwelling becomes unfit for continued occupation, then considerably more research is necessary. Clearly, each of the indexes includes an element of judgement and, if the indexes are to be entirely objective, attention will have to be paid to ways in which subjectivity and observer variability can be eliminated. Of more fundamental importance is the question of what constitutes tolerable living conditions and which conditions should be used as indices. In its publication *Appraisal of the Hygienic Quality of Housing and its Environment,* the World Health Organization (1967) lists examples of items for consideration in appraisal of rudimentary housing, conventional housing and the residential environment. In their attempts to evaluate neighbourhood quality, Lansing and Marans (1969) have demonstrated that a planner's perception of the desirable or undesirable features of an area may be different from those recognised by the residents. Clearly this opens up the whole philosophical/political question of whether the State has the right to dictate to its subjects the conditions under which it is fit for them to live. More important, perhaps, it focuses attention on the question of what items should be included in an assessment of housing quality and what conditions should be accepted as tolerable. If the individual has the right to certain minimum housing conditions, how and by whom should these conditions be determined?

CHAPTER 3
THE PROCESS OF OBSOLESCENCE:
THE PROBLEM OF CHANGING
LIFE-STYLES

The previous chapter began by pointing out that the problem of slum housing is the problem of accommodation which society deems to be unsuitable for continued occupation. To some, the problem can be resolved simply by eliminating all dwellings which are *currently* regarded as being unfit for habitation. This is not the case since 'our definition (whether statutory or interpretive) of what constitutes a slum will go on changing in response to rising standards and expectations.' (Watson, 1974, p. 62.) Dwellings, like other durable goods, are subject to the process of obsolescence.

CONCEPTS OF HOUSING OBSOLESCENCE

Obsolescence is the process by which operations or objects become obsolete; it is a transition state from full utility to complete uselessness. When a mode of operation or item of equipment is completely useless, it is said to be obsolete. However, opinions about degrees of utility 'vary according to the knowledge and viewpoint of the assessor and his awareness of possible alternative states and conditions' (Nutt, Walker, Holliday and Sears, 1976, pp. 5 and 6). Clearly interpretation of the terms 'obsolete' and 'obsolescence' is subjective and relative but it must be appreciated that any factor tending 'to reduce the ability or effectiveness of a building to meet the demands of its occupants, relative to other buildings in its class, will contribute towards the obsolescence of that building' (Nutt, Walker, Holliday and Sears, 1976, p. 6).

Buildings, both individual and as a group, have several important features; they are place-fixed, have long physical lives, entail exceedingly high levels of capital expenditure, are composed of many component parts and have a variety of functions. As a result, numerous factors can be identified which stimulate obsolescence. For instance, *style obsolescence*, the declining relative value of the visual appearance of a building or area has been identified by Meyerson, Terret and Wheaton (1962), while Little (1964) suggests that *structural* obsolescence occurs when a building becomes increasingly inadequate owing to the deterioration of its physical fabric. Since the equipment within buildings also becomes obsolete, Lowry (1960) has identified what he calls *technological obsolescence* while Kirby (1971) suggests that *social* or *functional obsolescence* occurs when a dwelling does not possess, or permit a household to possess, facilities and amenities which society regards as being essential for modern living, thereby rendering the dwelling increasingly unable to satisfy the life-styles of contemporary households. Medhurst and Parry Lewis (1969) suggest that *environmental obsolescence* occurs when conditions in a neighbourhood render it unfit for its current use.

Other types of obsolescence, such as *financial obsolescence* (Lichfield, 1968) have also been identified. Frequently, these relate more to the management and utilisation of the property rather than to a lessening in the use–efficiency of the property itself. While they may generate further obsolescence (through, for instance, reduced investment in maintenance) they are often based on an appraisal of the value of the property relative to other properties. In effect, therefore, they reflect an appraisal of the degree of obsolescence inherent in the property itself. This point is rarely made clear in the literature with the consequence that the concept of obsolescence becomes confused. Further confusion is generated by the differing objectives of the investigators and by the profusion of terms. Depending on their objectives, authors tend to place emphasis on differing aspects of obsolescence and to use different terms when discussing the same types.

Studies of obsolescence can be grouped into three categories. The early studies tended to view obsolescence as a physical process of deterioration and decay, while post-war studies have tended to concentrate on the economic life of buildings. More recent studies have adopted a behavioural approach although one of the most penetrating examples was published as early as 1933. In his paper 'Time zoning as a preventive of blighted areas', Lonberg-Holm (1933) suggests that the main factors causing building obsolescence are improvements in design, layout, structural and mechanical equipment, increasing mobility of population and production, socio-economic changes and physical deterioration. He argues that obsolescence is, in fact, an index of human progress and this line of argument is echoed in more recent studies. For instance, Cowan (1965), Jones (1967) and Kirby (1971) equate the development of functional obsolescence with the increasing misfit over time between activity requirements and building provisions, while most authors seem agreed that, if the quality of the environment is to be maintained, the forces of growth and change need to be understood. Accordingly, despite the differences in objectives and terminology, most authors would appear to agree that obsolescence can be regarded as 'a lessening of use efficiency resulting from the introduction or more desirable systems into the technology or social organization of human functions' (Kirby, 1971, p. 265).

THE PROCESS OF HOUSING OBSOLESCENCE

While several studies have attempted to describe the concept of obsolescence, few have tried to explain the process by which dwellings become obsolete. In any attempt to appreciate the process, attention must focus on the obsolescent article.

In their study of substandard housing in the United States, Hartman and Hook (1956) demonstrate that there is no statistically significant relationship between the age of a dwelling and its condition. Even so, a twofold link exists between physical decay and age. Throughout its life, the external structure of a dwelling is exposed to physical and chemical weathering, while the interior (in particular) suffers from the wear involved in the day-to-day use of the property by its inhabitants. The longer a dwelling is exposed to such treatment, the greater the damage and the more extensive the decay. Damage can be rectified, of course, by repair, while maintenance (properly planned and executed) can protect the property and retard decay. Dwellings all too frequently exhibit signs of neglect, however, and it would seem that this stems from the relatively low esteem in which the structure is held by the owner and/or the occupier.

In terms of the occupants (whether owner or tenant) this reduced level of esteem may result from the status of the household – a poor household may be too impoverished to care for the accommodation, while an old household may not desire the disturbance or discomfort which maintenance may entail or it may feel that its own life-expectancy does not warrant the appropriate expenditure. Alternatively, neglect may result from an attitude of mind towards structures in general (the occupant may show little, if any, concern for the condition of objects in his possession, whether they are owned by him or by others); accommodation relative to other structures (the occupant may show little concern for the state or condition of his accommodation though he may pay considerable attention to the maintenance of his car, garden, allotment, etc.) or towards the occupant's own accommodation relative to other accommodation (the tenant, for example, may not be prepared to care for his accommodation though he might if he owned it or if it provided a higher standard of accommodation, while the owner-occupier may not feel inclined to maintain his accommodation if the life expectancy of the property does not justify the investment). Occupants can be in any of these classes and can be spread through all standards of accommodation. However, given the constraints of finance, it might be assumed that the best quality property will be occupied by households which, for one reason or another, place considerable importance on the quality of their environment, while the poorer accommodation will tend to be occupied by those that do not. Such an assumption is basic to the traditional concept of housing filtering or passing down the social scale. As better property and more desirable areas are developed, the most mobile and discerning move to this accommodation, leaving behind dwellings which become occupied by families which are frequently unable or unwilling to undertake maintenance operations at the level to which they are required. Deterioration, of both the property and, frequently, the environment, occurs and further households move out, leaving behind the recent inhabitants, those unconcerned about the deterioration of their environment and those who are unable or unwilling to move.

Landlords, whether public or private, might be similarly classified but economic factors would seem to influence a great many. In many instances, particularly in the public sector (Kirby, 1972), it would seem that the returns from the property are insufficient to pay for proper and adequate maintenance. However, it is not unusual for the landlord, in an attempt to increase his income, to neglect maintenance or to divide the accommodation into smaller units. In either event, the result is, frequently, deterioration and the worse a property becomes, the lower the relative rent that can be charged and the less that can be spent on repairs. At the same time, the poorer the property, the more it is likely to be inhabited by households which are either unwilling or unable to undertake effective maintenance. The process is self-perpetuating and spreads to neighbouring properties until whole areas are affected.

Over time, therefore, most dwellings and residential environments deteriorate physically and experience a reduction in desirability. This reduction in desirability reflects a decline in the standard of accommodation provided by the property relative to newer structures and it would appear that (directly or indirectly) the neglect of maintenance that leads to decay is a reflection of lowered esteem for an obsolescent article. In most circumstances, obsolescence occurs when more efficient or desirable systems are introduced to the technology or social organisation of human functions. Occasionally, obsolescence can result from the introduction of a less desirable system as in the case, for instance, where the development of a non-residential land-use, lower income housing or the extension of an airport runway can initiate obsolescence of the residential environment. These changes (innovations) which initiate obsolescence can take the form of physical hardware (e.g. central heating systems, deep freezers, motor cars, etc.) or social *mores* (e.g. changes in attitude towards family size, communal living, female employment, etc.). In either form, their introduction affects the behaviour of households and, therefore, the demands which are placed upon both the dwelling and the environment.

When a dwelling, and/or the environment in which it is situated, fails to meet the activity demands of its occupants, the dwelling is said to be obsolete. Naturally, activity demands vary from household to household and though a dwelling fails to meet the requirements of one set of occupants, it may satisfy quite adequately the requirements of another. However, if the factors promoting failure are symptomatic of a change in general tendency, resulting from the adoption of innovation, then the accommodation is subject to obsolescence. For example, if a dwelling failed to meet the space require-ments of a particular set of occupants, it would not be obsolete unless it failed to meet the space requirements of all households. Similarly it would not be obsolete if its failure resulted from the size fluctuations which occur in the normal life-cycle of households. Obsolescence would be involved, however, if failure reflected a general tendency towards larger or smaller households or an increase or decrease in equipment or possessions.

It was pointed out earlier in this chapter that dwellings are subject to various forms of obsolescence. In his discussion of the mechanisms of the filtering concept, Lowry (1960) suggests that although a dwelling may fall below the standards of social adequacy because of technological obsolescence, the impact of this type of quality decline is greatly reduced because the current standards of social adequacy are so minimal. For Lowry (1960, p. 366), 'physical deterioration is probably the most important factor . . . in the emergence of substandard housing.' In contrast, Cowan (1965, p. 1 397) points out in his review of Ratcliffe's (1949) observations on obsolescence that 'because the rate of obsolescence of mechanical equipment is relatively high compared with that of building structures, with the increasing number of items of mechanical equipment contained in buildings, especially houses, the rate of obsolescence of structures is likely to rise in the future.' Clearly, the importance of technological obsolescence is perceived differently by the two authors. It is argued here that physical or technological obsoles-cence and social or functional obsolescence are the two most fundamental forms since both cause property to become unsuitable for continued habitation and both are the basis of, or are related to, all other forms. In each case they result from innovation and it is important not to confuse physical or technological obsolescence with structural dilapidation. The latter is a product of neglect while the former is a resultant of innovations in physical hardware. Physical or technological obsolescence occurs when the facilities provided by a dwelling or its environment are perceived to be functionally substandard relative to more recent installations. Similarly, functional or social obsoles-cence is the product of innovations in either hardware or social attitudes since it occurs when a dwelling or its environment does not possess, or permit a household to possess, facilities and amenities which society regards as being essential for modern living. In both instances, obsolescence results from the failure of either the dwelling or the residential environment to permit the pattern of behaviour that is regarded as conducive to modern living. In other words the dwelling and its environment are failing to satisfy the activity demands of contemporary households.

CONCLUSION

This relationship between innovation, changing household requirements and obsoles-cence has long been recognised in Britain. In 1918, for instance, the Tudor Walters

Committee observed that 'the general standard of accommodation and equipment demanded by the working classes has been rising for some time.' (Local Government Boards for England and Wales and Scotland, 1918, p. 8.) Accordingly it recommended that 'in the face of an improving standard, it is only wise economy to build dwellings which, so far as may be judged, will continue to be above the accepted minimum, at least for the whole period of the loan with the aid of which they are provided, say sixty years.' (Op. cit., p. 8.) Some forty-three years later, in 1961, the point was reiterated by the Parker Morris Committee in *Homes for Today and Tomorrow*. The Committee recognised that 'since the end of the war, the country has undergone a social and economic revolution and the pattern is still changing fast.' (Ministry of Housing and Local Government, 1961, p. 1.) Like the Tudor Walters Committee its solution was the recommendation of standards that would give reasonable satisfaction over the years and would 'be adequate to meet the newly emerging needs of the future, as well as the basic human needs which always stay the same' (op. cit., p. 2). However, 'Parker Morris standards are already obsolete long before they have been generally adopted' (Eversley, 1967, p. 1 338) and it has been demonstrated (Kirby, 1971) that, some thirty to fifty years after their construction, inter-war council dwellings were providing a standard of accommodation which, in many respects, might be perceived as being unsuitable for the latter half of the twentieth century. Both the Tudor Walters and Parker Morris Committees failed to counteract obsolescence because they were unable to anticipate the social, economic and technological changes which have occurred and the rate at which these changes have taken place. As Nutt *et al.* (1976, p. 25) have observed, 'this comprehensive notion of obsolescence is becoming established at a general conceptual level. Despite this, however, there are few research methods and operational techniques to help formalise and extend our understanding of obsolescence.' If long-life dwellings (with an estimated life span of sixty years or more) continue to be built, however, more attention will have to be paid to the process by which dwellings become obsolete and to the methods by which the rate of obsolescence can be retarded.

CHAPTER 4
THE FILTERING CONCEPT
AND NEW BUILDING

The previous chapters have examined the problems of slums and slum housing and stressed that the two sets of problems are not synonymous. No attention has yet been paid to the policies intended to resolve these problems. In this and the following two chapters attention will be paid to three of the most universally adopted approaches to the problem of slum housing, namely filtering, clearance and rehabilitation. Two of these, clearance and rehabilitation involve some form of Government intervention in the housing programme, usually subsidised new (or renovated) housing for lower or middle income households. Filtering, however, involves no such programme of direct intervention; no attempt is made to raise the general level of housing standards through the provision of accommodation for the poorer members of the community. Rather, the raising of housing standards is left to the free play of the market through the construction of new properties for the middle and upper income groups. As might be expected, the concept of filtering has played an important part in the formulation of housing policy in the United States of America. In his review of the various strategies for housing the urban poor, Downs (1969) has observed that since most subsidies have been to middle and upper income households, filtering has been the implicit, if not explicit, policy of the United States, despite its programme of public housing construction. Some would also argue that filtering is an integral part of British housing policy. Up to the early 1930s, Britain relied almost entirely upon the filtering process for improving the housing conditions of the working classes. Although housing subsidies had been available since 1919, they were intended, as Bowley (1945) has pointed out, to stimulate building in an inflationary period and to remedy the housing shortage. Once this had been achieved, it was believed that a return would be made to the free market. It was not until the Housing Act of 1930 and the Housing (Financial Provisions) Act of 1933 that the Government officially recognised that the housing problems of the lower income groups were not likely to be resolved by private building. As Macey and Baker (1973, p. 17) observe 'there may have been some filtering up by a proportion of the slum clearance tenants moving into houses vacated by those who went to 1924 Act houses, but the extent of this was slight. The slum clearance provisions of the 1923 Act were complex and difficult to operate. Conditions of depression were so bad, and incomes so low, that very little was being done for those most in need of help. To remedy this state of affairs the 1930 Act (known as the Greenwood Act) was passed.'

THE FILTERING PROCESS

Policies based on the filtering process utilise, directly, the concept of obsolescence. As new, more modern houses become available, they are purchased by households in the upper and middle income groups whose former dwellings are bought by households in the lower income groups. Thus a chain of sales in initiated by the construction of new dwellings for the upper classes and this chain results in the older properties filtering down the social scale while individual households filter up the housing scale thereby leaving the worst housing vacant and ready for demolition. This, very simply, is the filtering concept. As dwellings obsolesce, they become available to the lower income groups and provide, for them, an improved standard of accommodation. However, the analysis of filtering is largely an oral tradition and, as a consequence, 'the concept itself is fuzzy' (Lowry, 1960, p. 362). Although the concept of filtering is widely recognised, therefore, there is no universal agreement on a definition of the process. This is important since the definition used 'determines the selection of factors to be examined and influences the types of measurements to be made and conclusions to be reached' (Grigsby, 1963, p. 84).

Perhaps the four most widely accepted definitions are those of Ratcliffe, Fisher and Winnick, Lowry, and Grigsby. Each places different emphasis on the different market processes incorporated in the definition. In *Urban Land Economics,* Racliffe (1949, pp. 321–2) suggests that filtering 'is described most simply as the changing of occupancy as the housing that is occupied by one income group becomes available to the next lower income group as a result of decline in market price, i.e. sales price or rent value'. Clearly, for Ratcliffe, there are two separate and distinct elements – change in value and change in occupancy. For Fisher and Winnick (1951) these two elements result in confusion since the relationship between occupancy and price is not uniform. They demonstrate, for instance, that with rising real incomes, it is possible for a group of dwellings to be occupied by successively higher income groups although the relative value of the dwellings may have declined. For them, therefore, 'filtering . . . is a change in the position of a given dwelling unit or group of dwelling units within the distribution of housing prices and rents in the community as a whole' (Fisher and Winnick, 1951, p. 52). Clearly such a definition is not intended to be used to determine whether filtering supplies lower income groups with improved housing. Later in their analysis, however, Fisher and Winnick (1951, p. 53) point out that 'as newer units are added (generally at higher than average rents) the community standard is raised. . . . Demolition of the lowest priced (and presumably the poorest) housing will have a similar effect by raising the average quality of the housing inventory.' Even so, when commenting on the Fisher and Winnick definition, Lowry (1960) has suggested that the concept has been deprived of its analytical usefulness when considering the way in which the filtering process can produce a general improvement in housing conditions and bring improved living conditions within the reach of the lower income groups. Lowry's own definition is, simply, 'a change in the real value (price in constant dollars) of an existing dwelling unit' (Lowry, 1960, p. 363). He uses it to demonstrate that filtering is not a process which necessarily results in all families occupying housing above certain minimum standards. Olsen (1969) has modified the Lowry definition in an attempt to demonstrate more easily the result which Lowry showed with difficulty. He argues that if Lowry intended that money values should be deflated by the cost of construction, then a dwelling unit can only be regarded as having filtered if 'the quantity of housing stock contained in this unit has changed' (Olsen, 1969, p. 139). Filtering up would occur when the quantity of housing stock in the unit had increased whereas downward filtering would take place when the quantity of housing stock in the unit had decreased.

Since none of these definitions specifies that filtering produces better housing standards, Grigsby (1963) asserts that none would shed light on whether filtering facilitates an improvement in housing conditions. He argues that to do this, the definition would have to incorporate some measure of improvement in housing conditions. Accordingly, he suggests that 'filtering only occurs when value declines more rapidly than quality so that families can obtain either higher quality and more space at the same price or the same quality and space at a lower price than formerly' (Grigsby, 1963, p. 97).

It is clear, therefore, that there are several interpretations of the filtering process. This inevitably causes confusion although there seems to be broad agreement when the topic is discussed in casual conversation. While Grigsby (1963) maintains that each of the definitions is useful for a different purpose, there is little doubt that, when coupled with empirical evidence on chains of sales, arguments surrounding these various definitions have influenced attitudes towards the filtering concept in terms of its incorporation into policies directed at raising housing standards and bringing improved housing conditions within the reach of the lowest income groups.

EMPIRICAL STUDIES OF THE FILTERING PROCESS

In recent years, several studies have attempted to test the filtering process. In *Housing Markets and Public Policy,* Grigsby (1963) outlines the results of a study which analysed the 1956 National Housing Inventory data for Philadelphia. He found that movement for the rental to the owner-occupier market was in excess of movement in the opposite direction, though some 30 per cent of owners who moved went to rented accommodation. Movement into more expensive homes, however, was found to be more prevalent in the owner-occupier sector than in the rental sector and to be of most importance in the suburban home ownership market. Thus, the study revealed some evidence of the filtering process operating in the total housing market but found that it was particularly conspicuous in the sector of owner occupation. When the owner-occupier market was examined in more detail, it was revealed that approximately 40 per cent of former renters went to new homes, whereas over 45 per cent of former owners moved into used property. This would seem to suggest some conflict with the filtering model whereby households in rented accommodation might be expected to enter the home ownership market through the purchase of older property. The figures for the inner city reveal that new homes were purchased by only 11 per cent of those formerly living in rented accommodation as opposed to 75 per cent of those who had owned their previous accommodation. Thus the results seem to suggest that there is some evidence of the filtering process operating in the Philadelphia housing market. The study also revealed, however, that some 20 per cent of all moves in the owner occupier market were to less expensive dwellings and that, in the rental sector, filtering down the dwelling stock was as important as filtering up. It would appear, therefore, that in the Philadelphia housing market at least, downward filtering of households is not uncommon. Clearly, some households move to smaller, less expensive accommodation on the break-up of the family through marriage, death, etc. but it has been observed elsewhere that 'some families move because they can no longer afford their houses. It would appear that in both percentage and absolute numbers, those who move because of insufficient finances exceed those who move to upgrade their housing. . . .' (Maisel, 1966, p. 107.)

Further empirical evidence comes from the work of Lansing, Clifton and Morgan (1969). In their study *New Homes and Poor People* they attempt to test the filtering hypothesis by answering such related questions as 'what is the economic level of the people who move into new housing? If rich people move into new housing, do poor people benefit indirectly by moving into vacancies farther along in the sequence? Or do the sequences stop before they reach low income people?' (Lansing, Clifton and Morgan, 1969, p. 111).

To answer these questions, the researchers examined the chains of sales generated by the construction and occupation of new dwellings. They found that while the average length of chains begun by new housing was over four, this was doubled as the price of new housing increased from under $15 000 to over $30 000. Most sequences were found to have ended because the whole household did not leave the point of origin. Only 20 per cent of the chains were ended by demolition or conversion whereas 61 per cent were ended because the households which moved into a vacant dwelling had been living with their parents or other relatives, previously.

Even so, the survey revealed that households tended to move into better housing and that the socio-economic status of those moving into a dwelling tends to be lower than that of those moving out. The researchers found, for instance, that the median value of a new owner-occupied dwelling was $25 000 while it was only $18 000 for the property fifth in the sequence. Similarly, only 6 per cent of the households occupying new homes earned less that $3 000 per annum whereas the proportion was as high as 16 per cent for those living in the fifth unit in the chain. Moreover, some 55 per cent of those moving into a dwelling had lower incomes than the previous occupants. Even so, approximately 25 per cent had higher incomes and it would appear that the lower down the sequence, the greater the probability of the incoming household having a higher income than the household it replaced.

Clearly, there are considerable problems associated with the use of income as a measure of the filtering process – the incoming household may, for instance, have the same social or professional status as the outgoing household but be at an earlier stage in its professional career. Indeed, the survey revealed that in 41 per cent of the cases the outgoing family was in a later stage of the family life-cycle than the household that succeeded it. When completed education was used in place of income as a measure of socio-economic status, 40 per cent of the in-movers were of lower status than the out-movers but 32 per cent were ranked higher.

While the study showed that poor people do gain some benefit from new construction, the findings are generally inconclusive and, at best, the filtering process is shown to be only partly responsible for raising housing standards.

Guy and Nourse (1970) have examined the operation of the filtering process in two areas, Kankakee, Illinois, and Webster Groves, Missouri. In the former they examined the income of each household in two sample neighbourhoods over the period 1918–69. Here they found that the filtering process did occur in the long term but that its effects on a neighbourhood were gradual. Property was found to have filtered up and there were only a few years when filtering down was sufficiently in excess of filtering up to be statistically significant. In the latter area, Webster Groves, they took a sample of 138 addresses and examined the change in occupancy for each address from 1926–69. In addition, they attempted to determine whether the household moving into the dwelling had the same income as the outgoing household when it first moved in and to assess the effect of changes in the income of occupants over time. Obviously a rise in income might stimulate a household to upgrade its accommodation while a drop in income might force a move to a less expensive home. However, neither upward nor downward filtering can be said to occur unless the real income of the outgoing household at the time it first occupied the dwelling is different from that of the present occupants at initial occupation. On this basis, they found that there had been no significant filtering down in the community over the period studied and in only one neighbourhood was it possible to reject the null hypothesis that filtering up was equal to filtering down. It is recognised by the researchers, however, that it is 'common knowledge in the real estate market of St Louis that Webster is a relatively stable community' (Guy and Nourse, 1970, p. 45). Perhaps the same study could have produced different results in another area.

CONCLUSION

In theory, then, the filtering process should work towards the elimination of slum conditions. With the construction of new housing for the upper income groups, upward filtering occurs and the low income slum residents move into the non-slum homes vacated by the wealthier sectors of the urban community. Empirical research evidence on the effectiveness of filtering would seem to be inconclusive and there exists a distinct need for research into the residential aspirations and mobility patterns of slum dwellers. In reality, there are several reasons why the filtering process should not raise housing standards and meet, automatically, the needs of successively lower income groups. In the first place, the housing market is more complex than the filtering concept might suggest. It has been observed elsewhere that 'in practice, the dynamics of the housing market can probably best be viewed as a combination of "blow out" and "filter down".' (Harvey, 1973, p. 173.) Under the blow out theory, social and physical pressures are exerted at the bottom end of the housing market and transmitted up the socio-economic scale until the richest households are pressured to move. Since the richest households will not move unless they prefer to, the various intermediate groups are squeezed between a social pressure emanating from below and an immovable political and economic force above. Harvey cites the evidence of Smith (1966) as support for the blow out theory. Smith found that it was the middle and lower income groups that took up new housing in Los Angeles while the upper income groups remained stationary or filtered in to older housing in good locations.

A further reason for the failure of the filtering process to eliminate slums is the fact that 'the price decline necessary to bring a dwelling unit within reach of an income group lower than that of the original tenants also results in a policy of undermaintenance.' (Lowry, 1960, p. 370.) Clearly, if this is the case, the policy of price decline basic to the filtering concept would not raise housing standards but would produce deterioration of the housing stock. In addition, the difference in the size distribution of the various income groups would work against households filtering up the social scale. Since the higher income groups constitute a relatively small class, the houses they vacate in preference for new buildings are demanded by a much larger group. As a consequence, the resultant price reduction is kept to a minimum if it occurs at all. Because of this, it would appear that 'the lower in the price scale at which it is possible to inject new houses, the greater will be the benefit to lower income families.' (Cullingworth, 1966. p. 266.) This is now generally accepted and in many countries, government policy is increasingly directed at providing housing assistance to the underprivileged. However, in a theoretical consideration of multipliers, vacancy chains and filtering, White (1971, p. 92) argues that subsidised low income housing is not the most effective method of 'improving the overall match of families' needs with available houses'. Certainly the provision of only low income housing limits upward filtering to the low income groups but, as Yeates and Garner (1971, p. 285) observe 'the ethical morality of providing new housing for only the wealthy . . . is dubious' and perhaps the best policy is to provide new housing for all income groups.

CHAPTER 5
CLEARANCE AND REBUILDING

The demolition of substandard or obsolete housing and the construction of new property is one of the most important methods of eliminating bad housing conditions and improving the general standard of the housing stock. As a consequence, it constitutes a relatively long-established feature of the housing policies of most Western societies. As mentioned previously, for instance, the British Government introduced a policy of slum clearance under the 1930 Housing Act, while in America a programme of renewal was initiated by the Housing Act of 1949. Several authors (Davis, 1960; Elks, 1972; Marris, 1962) have pointed out, however, that clearance programmes can have a number of objectives and the elimination of blight and improvement of housing conditions are only two of these. Others include the revival of downtown business areas, the maintenance of an adequate middle income component in the central area, the strengthening of the city tax base, etc. Accordingly, it is important to appreciate at the outset that 'these aims are neither the same nor necessarily compatible.' (Marris, 1962, p. 182). It is also important to appreciate that, even where the objectives are the same, the mechanisms utilised to achieve these objectives may be different and the implications of clearance programmes may differ from one area or society to another. Thus although the American Housing Act of 1949 initiated a clearance programme similar in its objectives to that initiated by the British Housing Act of 1930, the two programmes contrast markedly in the mechanisms for achieving these objectives and relocating slum dwellers in 'decent, safe and sanitary' housing. The difference between the British and American policies is that, as it was pointed out in the previous chapter, American housing policy relies heavily upon filtering; the American policy is one of clearance whereas the policy followed by Britain and other European countries is that of clearance and rehousing. In Britain, and elsewhere in Europe, relatively low-cost housing is built and managed by the various local government authorities. When an area of slum housing is to be cleared, the residents are offered accommodation in property owned by the local authority. In America, however, there is a limit on the number of dwellings that can be constructed in the public sector each year and while authorities are required to 'ensure that decent, safe and sanitary housing is available to the families relocated' (Marris, 1962, p. 182) they are not required to provide this accommodation. As a consequence, although there are similarities in the physical and social impact of clearance programmes in the two countries, there are also distinct differences and these differences have to be borne in mind when attempting to assess the success and social implications of clearance.

Fig. 5.1 The demolition of substandard housing and the construction of new property is one of the most important methods of eliminating bad housing conditions (SHELTER picture library).

THE IMPACT OF CLEARANCE

America

In his study of the relocation of the slum residents of Boston's West End, Hartmann (1964, p. 275) concludes that the American clearance programme 'has made a disappointingly small contribution to the attainment of "a decent home in a suitable living environment for every American family" '. Several studies have attempted, in fact, to assess the contribution of clearance to the elimination of slum housing and although the results seem to vary from project to project, the overall impression is one of limited achievement.

One of the major objectives of clearance is, quite clearly, to improve the living conditions of slum dwellers. In his analysis of the achievements of the American urban renewal programme over the period, 1914–62, Anderson (1964) found that many areas had been cleared to permit the expansion of hospitals, libraries, colleges, etc. and the development of luxury housing projects which the dispossessed slum dwellers could not afford. As a consequence, a 1961 survey of clearance programmes in forty-one American cities revealed that some 60 per cent of the dispossessed households had merely been relocated in other slums. A similar conclusion is reached by Hartmann (1964) in his study of the relocation of slum dwellers living in the West End of Boston. Hartmann demonstrates that only 73 per cent of the residents were relocated in good housing and points to the discrepancy which exists between this and the official figure of 97 per cent. Gans (1965, p. 30) suggests that the discrepancy may have arisen from the fact that 'renewal officials collected their data after the poorest of the uprooted tenants had fled in panic to the other slums and that officials also tended toward a rather lenient evaluation of the relocation housing . . . in order to make a good record for their agency.' Marris (1962) also refers to the fact that relocation authorities tend to be more optimistic than independent enquirers and claims that between 15 and 50 per cent of the households affected by clearance still live in substandard housing. He also points out that in most cities less than 10 per cent of the households were relocated in public sector housing though a higher proportion would have been eligible for such accommodation. The overall conclusion seems to be that most households move to neighbourhoods similar to those from which they have been moved. Usually these areas are on the fringe of the clearance area and often they are areas scheduled for clearance in the near future. For instance, in a survey of 709 households moving from public housing sites to private housing, New York City Planning Commission found that 49 per cent moved into areas scheduled for future redevelopment. There is no mechanism in America whereby the authorities can ensure that displaced households do not relocate in future clearance areas and attempts to introduce such a system would only make worse the already difficult task of finding suitable accommodation. For many, therefore, relocation means 'no more than keeping one step ahead of the bulldozer' (Hartmann, 1964, p. 278).

It would appear that the majority of American slum dwellers achieve no more than a marginal improvement in their housing as a result of clearance. Some move to other slum dwellings and many more move to nearby areas which, as Gruen (1963) argues, are likely to deteriorate quite rapidly into new slums. Even so, every relocation study from the early 1930s to the present reports an increase in rents. Hartmann (1964) found, for instance, that the move from the West End of Boston resulted in median monthly rents increasing from $41 to $71, while the median rent/income ratio rose from 13.6 per cent in the West End to 18.6 per cent after relocation. By comparison, Marris (1962) suggests that clearance brings about a rent increase of between $12 and $20 on average and has resulted in the proportion of income spent on rent increasing from approximately 17 to 25 per cent. Despite the differences in detail, researchers seem to be agreed that clearance programmes have resulted in widespread increases in housing costs and that these have occurred irrespective of any improvement in housing conditions and without any consideration of the ability or desire of households to absorb these costs. As might be expected, the residents of clearance areas are among the poorest members of society and although the classic studies have been carried out in old-style ethnic neighbourhoods such as the West End of Boston or the Back-of-the-Yards, Chicago, the majority of clearance areas are occupied not by Italians or Poles but by Negroes. Indeed, 'the more outspoken critics have come to refer scornfully to urban renewal as "Negro removal", implying that Negroes have special cause to be negative toward urban renewal.' (Barresi and Lindquist, 1970, p. 278.) Certainly, as the studies of racially mixed relocation indicate, the effects of discrimination make it even more difficult and expensive for the non-whites to obtain decent housing. As Hartmann (1964) points out, the most unsatisfactory relocation results, in terms of increased rents and the quality of housing, are in predominantly- or all-Negro areas.

American clearance programmes would appear, therefore, to have worsened, rather than improved, the social problems of many displaced households. Those households which relocate satisfactorily tend to be those with adequate financial, personal and social resources and those which view forced relocation as an opportunity to obtain the kind of housing they have desired for some time. This would suggest that clearance is resulting in a rich get richer, poor get poorer effect since those households with inadequate incomes and personal or social deficiencies appear to be those which have failed to improve their housing conditions and had difficulty absorbing the increases in housing expenditure. Throughout America, very little attention has been paid to the welfare of the households displaced by clearance. Rarely has the amount of time and effort spent on investigating and condemning slum housing been matched by corresponding interest in the fate of the households involved. Indeed, from 1949–64 only one-half of 1 per cent of the $2.2 billion federal expenditure on urban renewal was spent on the relocation of displaced households.

England and Wales

In his critique of the American urban renewal programme, Gans (1965, p. 32) argues that the solution 'is not to repeal urban renewal, but to transform it from a program of slum clearance and rehabilitation into a program of urban rehousing' – to build low- and medium-cost housing and to help slum dwellers move into this property. This approach is commonplace in many European countries and has been practised in England and Wales since the early 1930s. As Bowley (1945) has pointed out, however, the greatest benefit from subsidised housing is frequently felt by the better-off in the lower income groups rather than the poorest sections of the population. Accordingly, the British slum clearance programme has been criticised, like the American programme, because most slum dwellers 'do not find themselves on a spanking new estate . . . but in another condemned or soon-to-be-condemned area of housing' (Harrison, 1972, p. 7). There are several reasons why this should be: some households move before the authority has chance to offer accommodation, some do not qualify for rehousing since they are not authorised tenants, while others believe they will be unable to afford the rents demanded by the authority for the dwellings it provides. Evidence from a sample survey in the St Mary's Ward of Oldham, Lancashire, indicates that about 90 per cent of the households in the clearance area were rehoused by the council and the Government suggests 'that this balance between those who rehoused themselves and those who became council tenants, is not unusual' (Ministry of Housing and Local Government,

1970b, p. 16). Earlier in the same report, the Government also recognises that many households, knowing that their houses were due for demolition, left the area before clearance began. It is not clear whether these households have been included in the official estimates. If they have not, then perhaps the proportion of households rehoused by the authorities is somewhat lower than 90 per cent. Certainly this would fit the evidence from Leeds where Wilkinson and Sigsworth (1963) found that only 70 per cent of the 917 households in their sample showed a desire for local authority accommodation. In 1970–71 Hull City corporation rehoused 88.3 households in council property for every 100 dwellings it demolished (City and County of Kingston-upon-Hull, 1971).

The results of the Government inquiry into the effect of redevelopment in the St Mary's area of Oldham reveal that most (67.5 per cent) of those households which rehoused themselves moved into privately rented, substandard accommodation less than 1 mile from their former homes. The majority were from the lowest income groups in the sample and most were found to be elderly single- or two-person households or large families dependent on a single income. Most opted out of the authority's rehousing programme because they felt they would be unable to afford the appropriate rent but a number wanted to remain near friends and relatives. While most of the households recognised the disadvantages of the dwellings they had moved to, they were probably just as unaware of the fact that many were likely to be cleared in future redevelopment programmes as were their counterparts in America. Generally it was found that moving had brought about a slight increase in rents, usually in the order of £0.50 and £0.75 per week. Prior to moving, however, most of the tenants in St Mary's Ward had been paying a weekly rent of less than £1.00 which would suggest that in many cases rents almost doubled as a result of the move.

Those households which had bought property had also tended to remain in the locality of their former homes for similar reasons. Although the standard of their accommodation was generally superior to that of those in privately rented accommodation, their housing costs were considerably higher and had normally involved a considerable increase when compared with the expenditure on their former homes. Two-thirds had paid deposits ranging from £50 to £400 and the majority had spent more than £40 on new floor coverings, curtains, furniture, etc.

Most of the St Mary's households that became council tenants were moved to post-war housing estates on the periphery of the town. By comparison, slum clearance households in Batley, Leeds and York were rehoused in dwellings which 'ranged in age from new completions to those produced in the inter-war period' (Wilkinson and Talbot, 1971, p. 241). The type and standard of council housing available to slum clearance households varies from authority to authority according to the range of property available and, more important, the allocation policy of the authority. When council house and slum clearance programmes were first developed in Britain, it was believed that improved housing conditions would produce improved behaviour patterns. As the President of the Local Government Board, John Burns, pointed out in the House of Commons debate on the 1908 Housing, Town Planning, etc. Bill, the object was 'to provide a domestic condition for the people in which their physical health, their morals, their character and their whole social condition can be improved'. Since the Second World War, this belief, with its roots in the philanthropic model communities of the nineteenth century, has been severely challenged. While social scientists have questioned the concept of environmental determinism and the desirability of 'improving' behaviour patterns, housing management has questioned the wisdom of accommodating 'problem' families in new property. In 1956, local authorities were advised that rehousing in a new house may not be the best thing for families unable or unwilling to attempt a better standard of living. These families 'are better placed in an old house, even if they have to be rehoused again within a few years' (Central Housing Advisory Committee, 1956, p. 13). Accordingly, many local authorities now follow a policy of grading tenants and allocating the poorest property to the poorest families. It is not easy to get authorities to admit to such a policy but details of these schemes are provided in several publications including Tucker's 1966 publication *Honourable Estates*. In his paper 'Selection and allocation in council housing', Gray (1976) provides a detailed outline of the procedure adopted by the Hull City Corporation. 'All new tenants are interviewed by a "housing investigator" before they move into Corporation housing. The investigator completes a form, taking details of the characteristics of the household and its present accommodation, the sort of dwelling and estate preferred and so on. The official also inspects the rent book and assesses the "condition of furniture" and "type of applicant". . . . A major function of the interview is to determine how good a tenant the applicant will be and the completed form becomes the instrument for deciding the type of accommodation to be offered to the household.' (Gray, 1976, p. 41.) Through an analysis of the investigator's forms, Gray demonstrates that the quality of property occupied is strongly related to the status of the household as determined by the authority. High status households in Hull have a good chance of being allocated a new local authority house while tenants with an intermediate status will probably be allocated a post-war house and low status households will be directed to pre-war housing. Given the characteristics of slum dwellers, it is to be expected that in many areas, the residents of slums will find themselves rehoused in the oldest of the council's accommodation. Even so, pre-war council dwellings do provide a relatively high standard of accommodation when compared with much older property (Kirby, 1971; Powell, 1974) and for the majority of slum dwellers it is likely to be a distinct improvement on their previous accommodation.

As in America, however, the move from a clearance area is likely to involve the household in increased living costs. The evidence from St Mary's Ward, Oldham, suggests that only 3 per cent of those households that moved into council accommodation paid the same, or a lower, rent as previously and for 49 per cent of the households rents and rates increased by over £1.00 per week. These increases were found to be causing financial difficulty for some households, particularly the large, young families and those households living on old age pensions. In addition, some households found their new home more costly to run and many found that the journeys to work, school and shops were not only less convenient but also more costly. Similar findings were reported by Wilkinson and Talbot (1971) in their survey of rehousing in Batley, Leeds and York. On average, the direct costs of moving amounted to approximately £68 which, as the researchers observe, was a sizeable amount for people with an average income of between £15 and £17 per week. Rent and rates were found to have increased by between £0.50 and £3.00 per week and about half of the households found that the move involved increases in heating and lighting. As in Oldham, the old age pensioners were the hardest hit but the researchers found that although adjustments to budgets had been necessary in the majority of cases, most households did not regard them as excessive. Indeed, both studies found that despite initial opposition to the move, there was a high level of satisfaction among those families rehoused by the various councils – most households felt they had gained from the move. Explanations for this are numerous; some respondents may not wish to reveal their true feelings to researchers, particularly representatives of the Government, some may be hiding behind a front and trying to convince themselves as well as others that the move has been beneficial, while for others, fear of the unknown might well have created an initial reaction to the move – a reaction which disappeared shortly after the move took place. Regardless of the reasons, the official view seems to be that the evidence does not 'suggest that a move to a new type of dwelling results in less satisfaction' (Ministry of Housing and Local Government, 1970b, p. 20).

PERSONAL AND COMMUNITY DISRUPTION

While differences exist in the mechanisms and impact of clearance in Britain and America, there is little disagreement between social scientists on either side of the Atlantic regarding the disruptive effect of clearance on the individual and the community. As Barnes (1974, p. 38) points out 'to be faced, at whatever age, with the sudden necessity of moving and usually without the resources to exercise much choice in the matter, is a truly traumatic experience. It is a shock which takes a lot of getting over. . . .' This is particularly true in the case of the involuntary relocations brought about by clearance. In Chapter 1 it was pointed out that many slum dwellers lack the personal resources to cope with the everyday pressures of life while others have sought the anonymity of slum life. For these households in particular, involuntary relocation can stimulate a serious psychological condition. It is not surprising to discover in 'Grieving for a lost home', for instance, that Fried (1963) reports that 46 per cent of the women and 38 per cent of the men from Boston's West End displayed a fairly severe grief reaction when questioned about leaving the West End. What is surprising, perhaps, is the fact that, far from adjusting to this trauma, 26 per cent of the women remained sad or depressed up to two years later. This situation is worsened by two additional factors – the destruction of the slum community and the uncertainty and delays which frequently surround clearance programmes.

In America, as the previous section has shown, major rehousing programmes rarely exist and frequently clearance results in the dispersal of slum dwellers to several locations in the urban area. In Britain, the early clearance schemes involved the construction of estates specifically intended for the tenants of clearance areas (Kirby, 1974a). Such a procedure was contrary to the concept of the urban neighbourhood which dominated planning thought in Britain throughout the 1950s and early 1960s. The aim of neighbourhood planning was to divide new and established urban areas into units which would allow the full growth of community spirit. Authorities were advised that a neighbourhood should not exceed a population of 10 000 persons but should be socially balanced, that is, it should be 'inhabited by families belonging to different ranges of income groups . . .' (Central Housing Advisory Committee, 1944, p. 61). The intention was that heterogeneity would add demographic balance, promote tolerance of social and cultural differences, provide a broader educational experience and, perhaps most important, encourage the lower classes to 'better' themselves. Further support for the break-up of communities came from those responsible for the management of Britain's local authority housing. It was argued that 'it is a mistake to rehouse too many problem families in one street. They generally have a bad effect upon each other and they will almost inevitably cause discomfort and resentment among their neighbours.' (Central Housing Advisory Committee, 1956, p. 13.) Since the Second World War, therefore, clearance programmes in Britain have also tended to bring about a dispersion of established slum communities. As a consequence, slum dwellers in both Britain and America have been deprived of the emotional support and informal patterns of mutual help and tolerance which characterise slum communities at the one time in their lives when they are required.

By adopting a deliberate policy of dispersion of slum dwellers throughout the urban area and bringing them into contact with non-slum households, it was anticipated that the social problem of the slums would be diluted and the former slum dwellers would be encouraged to 'better' themselves. The evidence would seem to suggest, however, that such a policy merely heightens the social and psychological problems of the relocated households. As Marris (1962, p. 183) observes, 'Neurotics and psychotics whose eccentricities were harboured, if not loved, in the slum streets, find themselves rejected in primmer neighbourhoods. Adolescents whose fear of the wider society was protected by the subculture of the slums become lost and unhappy.' What is more, this sort of reaction seems to occur even when households with similar backgrounds and status levels are brought together. In a study of the rehousing of households living in overcrowded or slum conditions in a Scottish burgh, for instance, Hole (1959, p. 163) found that 'those rehoused for overcrowding sometimes complained when families from condemned property were put beside them on the estate, saying that such tenants would lower the "respectable" tone of the neighbourhood. . . .' Again, it is interesting to examine the developments which have occurred in the Park Hill/Hyde Park complex in Sheffield. These are outlined by Darke and Darke (1972) in their article 'Sheffield revisited'. Previously a notorious slum, Park Hill/Hyde Park is a high rise housing area providing accommodation in continuous building form for 2 309 households. Although the two schemes are physically separate and Hyde Park (1 317 dwellings) is larger than Park Hill (992), the overall design is the same and the design principles are identical – to create a traditional working-class environment and to stimulate the development of 'community' spirit. From the evidence available, it would apppear that Park Hill does seem to have a sense of community and to have achieved the architect's objectives of something akin to the traditional working-class community. However, the housing manager's report for 1970–71 indicates that welfare, maintenance and management pressures seem to be relatively greater in Hyde Park which appears to have been less successful in terms of neighbourliness and community spirit. Given the physical similarities of the two schemes, the explanation for these social differences would appear to revolve around the radical differences in the structure and background of the tenants. At Park Hill, the first residents were mainly older, established households from slum clearance areas, two areas providing half of the tenants. On the other hand, Hyde Park was tenanted from the housing list mainly with young households who were unlikely to have known many families on the estate when they moved. Darke and Darke (1972, p. 56) conclude, therefore, that while the increased size of Hyde Park may have exacerbated these differences 'the Park Hill scheme benefited from the strong bonds which must have already existed between its tenants before they moved'. The Park Hill/Hyde Park example would seem to point to the case for not disrupting the slum community but rehousing it as a whole. Certainly the differences in the findings of the various studies of the social implications of clearance (Hole, 1959; Morris and Mogey, 1965; Ministry of Housing and Local Government, 1970b; Young and Willmott, 1962) seem to emphasise this point. Indeed, Morris and Mogey (1965, p. 162) conclude that the differences between their findings and those of Hole (1959) in Scotland are 'due to the fact that the Field Farm families were rehoused on the spot among familiar neighbours whereas the Scottish families were moved to a new area and set among strangers'.

Slum clearance is a complex and lengthy process and the delay and uncertainty which frequently surround clearance programmes only exacerbates the disruptive effect of relocation. In Britain, for instance, it takes about two years for a compulsory purchase order to be confirmed and another two years for the majority of the residents to be rehoused. In the years prior to the confirmation of the order, repair and maintenance

Fig. 5.2 The windows of an empty house are extremely attractive to small boys with bricks (SHELTER picture library).

work virtually cease since the owner recognises that the property (whether publicly or privately owned) is soon to be demolished. By the time the residents are eventually rehoused, therefore, 'their homes and the state of the surrounding streets are naturally far worse than when the public health inspectors represented the homes as unfit, two years or more previously' (Gee, 1974, p. 6). In the majority of cases, the period between the cessation of maintenance and rehousing is considerably longer than four years. Inevitably the programme is delayed and invariably maintenance ceases prior to the compulsory purchase order being issued. Frequently, the decision to clear an area is made some five to ten years before an order is issued and although most authorities keep their clearance programmes secret, it often becomes obvious that clearance is probable. Public services to an area are frequently reduced to a minimum, while the council often buys up property and leaves it empty. As Barnes (1974, p. 38) so vividly observes, there are four types of 'creatures' that take notice as soon as a house becomes empty. 'First . . . there are the squatters . . . Second, there are the flytippers: an unused garden is a very enticing place to empty rubbish, especially if the official place is some way off. Third, there are the vandals: the windows of an empty house are extremely attractive to small boys with bricks and, after the initial pleasure of the sound of breaking glass, the attractions to hide and seek, and loot, inside, are altogether overpowering. Where the young have pioneered, the older will follow to remove lead, copper, brass and anything else of value. Finally, there are the rats and mice, attracted by the rubbish, given a free run by the open doors and windows and the gaps left by wrenched out pipes but bringing (if not carefully controlled) grave dangers of disease.'

Clearly such physical conditions can have a demoralising psychological effect on the residents. They can also reinforce the cohesive structure of the community. As Pahl (1975, p. 49) observes 'different groups are knit into a cohesive structure through conflict.' Often, therefore, the fight against deteriorating living conditions and the common fear and uncertainty about the future brings even greater unity to the area – a unity which rehousing gradually, insidiously destroys. For a number of reasons, clearance rarely takes place at once and residents find that they are left without friends and relatives as households move or are moved, from the area. In the Shelter report on slum clearance, Gee (1974, p. 21) cites the case of a sixty-year-old woman from the St Peter's area of Newcastle upon Tyne. 'She had been born in her street; her brother also lived in the street, but only five other families still lived there. She was worried about whether she would ever get near her family again; worried about leaving the house to go on holiday because of the vandals breaking in while she was away; worried about her own health; was not sleeping; couldn't be bothered to do her own housework, hated going into her house, spent her time at home crying about her house and remembering how the street used to be when she was a girl and a young wife. She visited our office regularly (perhaps twice a week) and usually cried while there. On one occasion she was extremely upset, she had gone out shopping as usual and found herself running terrified down the street and crying. She had been passing the Co-op which she had known all her life and as she passed part of it was being pulled down. . . .'

Part of this woman's distress stemmed, quite obviously, from the insecurity generated by the physical and social destruction of the community in which she had spent her life – from the loss of friends and relatives and the disappearance of the familiar, reassuring features of her environment. There can be little doubt, however, that this sense of insecurity was compounded by her uncertainty and fear of the future. 'As planning gets under way, rumours are spread, arousing fear and insecurity among people who think they will be forced out of their homes at some indefinite future date. It is important to alleviate these fears as well as to achieve genuine citizen participa-

Fig. 5.3 The fight against deteriorating living conditions brings even greater unity to the slum (SHELTER picture library).

tion. . . .' (Montgomery, 1960, p. 405.) Unfortunately, as the above quotation and the Shelter report on slum clearance (Gee, 1974) demonstrate, both British and American clearance programmes fail, all too frequently, to provide the residents with accurate and timely information about the future of their homes.

Fig. 5.4 The new area takes on the social and, frequently, the physical characteristics of a slum (SHELTER picture library).

CONCLUSION

Most commentators seem agreed that while slum clearance may have made a positive contribution to the raising of housing standards, it has achieved little in terms of improving the overall circumstances of the slum dweller. In certain cases, slum households have been moved to improved accommodation, but in others they have been relocated in neighbourhoods little different from those from which they have been cleared. Whatever the case, the general tendency has been for the new area to take on the social and, frequently, the physical characteristics of a slum. What is more, the various research studies seem to suggest 'that the deleterious effects of the uprooting experience, the loss of familiar places and persons and the difficulties of adjusting to and accepting new living environments may be more serious issues than are changes in housing status' (Hartmann, 1964, p. 279). There is evidence to suggest, however, that where whole communities have been rehoused and efforts have been made to meet the social needs of the community, there has tended to be less dissatisfaction and less social failure than where there has been little or no attempt to implement such a comprehensive solution. Unfortunately, rarely have new housing projects been linked with resettlement services and social welfare programmes and slum households have been deprived of the mutual aid of their neighbours at a time when they were most required. Rather than being reduced by relocation, the social problems of many slum households would appear to have been increased. This being the case, it is difficult to disagree with Montgomery's (1960, p. 407) conclusion that 'relocation cannot be successful until the nation and its communities firmly determine to provide the health and welfare resources needed for human renewal. . . .'

CHAPTER 6
HOUSING REHABILITATION

Rehabilitation has long been recognised as a means of improving the quality of accommodation and eliminating slums. In America, for instance, the potential value of rehabilitation was recognised in the 1930s (Walker, 1938) while in Britain the first publicly assisted programme for the improvement of old houses was introduced as early as 1919 (Pepper, 1971). It was not until the 1960s, however, that significant emphasis was placed upon rehabilitation in either country. There are several possible reasons for this but before embarking on an examination of the various advantages and disadvantages of rehabilitation, perhaps it is pertinent to examine the scope and nature of the process.

Housing rehabilitation means different things to different people. 'To a homeowner, it encompasses everything from repairing the roof to changing a lightbulb. To a contractor it is the gutting and reconstruction of a home's interior. To an apartment owner, it is any improvement which allows him to increase the rents he receives. And to an economist, it is any investment designed to forestall the capital depreciation of a structure.' (Bagby, 1973, p. 1.) As a consequence, numerous definitions exist. In *The Dynamics of Housing Rehabilitation*, Listokin (1973, p. 4) cites several American definitions. He points out, for instance, that Osgood and Zwerner (1960) define rehabilitation 'as the elimination of environmental and structural deficiences which if not adequately and timely corrected, would result in neighbourhood blight' while Hendy (1970) 'viewed it as making a run-down uninhabitable building habitable' and Haas (1962) sees it as 'residential rebuilding to prevent obsolescence or diminishing utility and to restore safe, sound and sanitary standards'. Listokin sites several other definitions but between them, these three cover the main points relating to rehabilitation. Individually, however, they are inadequate. The definition by Osgood and Zwerner is inadequate since it seems to exclude property which can be regarded as being obsolete already. A similar criticism might be levelled at the definition by Hass but a much more fundamental criticism of this and Hendy's definition is the exclusion of any reference to the environment of the dwelling. As Chapter 2 revealed, a dwelling can be regarded as being unsuitable for habitation if the environment in which it is situated is unsatisfactory. Accordingly, a more appropriate definition of rehabilitation might be *residential rebuilding to eliminate the environmental and structural deficiencies which cause a dwelling to be regarded as being obsolete or sufficiently obsolescent as to be unsuitable for continued habitation*.

Several levels of rehabilitation exist. In America, for instance, the New York State Temporary State Housing Rent Commission differentiates between '*Code compliance* – such work as is necessary to restore the structure to safe and sanitary maintenance and

Fig. 6.1 (above and opposite) Rehabilitation has long been recognised as a means of improving the quality of accommodation and eliminating slums (GLC photographs).

repair ... *Minimal rehabilitation* – in addition to all work called for under code compliance, modest measures to upgrade the housing would include improvement in the outside appearance of the building and an increase in electrical capacity within the apartments. *Modernisation* – in addition to the work of minimal rehabilitation, outmoded mechanical equipment and fixtures would be replaced and all public areas of the building would be redecorated. No change in floor plans is included. *Remodelling* – floor layouts would be functionally rearranged to produce a large number of separate apartments than presently exist. Outmoded mechanical equipment would be replaced and the interior and exterior of the building would also be cleaned and painted as with modernisation.' (Listokin, 1973, p. 5.)

Similar levels can be recognised in Britain where improvement grants are given for various types of modernisation. *Standard grants* are available for the provision of seven standard or basic amenities. These include the provision of a fixed bath, or shower, hand-basin and sink and the provision of a hot and cold water supply to each, plus the installation of a water closet. In addition, *discretionary improvement* grants are paid for any improvement work to a dwelling which the local authority regards as raising the general standard of accommodation of the dwelling. Unlike the standard grant which relates to a small number of specific amenities, there are no specific improvements which qualify for grant aid and the local authority has complete discretion over the nature of the improvement work it recognises. However, the improved accommodation must comply with the 'twelve point' standard laid down under the Housing (Financial Provisions) Act of 1958. Further improvement grant aid is available for work providing residential accommodation through the conversion of a non-residential building or, more frequently, the division of a large house into smaller units. Finally, special amenity

grants are paid for non-revenue-producing environmental improvements. Clearly, therefore, there are various levels of rehabilitation and rehabilitation programmes vary according to a complex range of physical, economic, social and political factors. This might be anticipated in the private sector where different owners will have different attitudes towards improvement and modernisation. It is also true of the public sector, however, and in Britain there is considerable variation, between local authorities, over the modernisation of the accommodation built and owned by the authorities themselves (Kirby, 1974b).

Since variations exist in the nature of rehabilitation, it is only to be expected that differences will occur in the process by which rehabilitation is executed. Frequently, modernisation/improvement work is effected as part of the maintenance or repair routine but the concept of rehabilitation implies a positive, comprehensive programme. The principal types of rehabilitation are *renovation* and *wreckout*. Renovation involves preserving as much of the existing dwelling as possible but with wreckout the interior of the dwelling is completely gutted, irrespective of the condition of its individual components. Naturally, the choice of strategy is influenced by several factors including, perhaps, the quality of the original structure, the requirements of the intended occupants, the amount of capital available, etc. In turn, the choice of strategy affects several other factors including the quality of accommodation provided and the social benefits of rehabilitation over clearance and rebuilding.

SOCIAL ASPECTS

As Montero (1968, p. 17) observes, 'the rehabilitation of buildings in urban areas for low-rent housing cannot be thought of merely or simply as an inexpensive or easy way to provide housing facilities. The overall reason for rehabilitation must be social.' Indeed, the most persuasive case for rehabilitation is the argument that modernisation produces less social disruption than replacement. It is argued that families are not forced to move away from their accustomed surroundings and are not faced with more difficult and costly journeys to work, shop and school: the community is maintained and the pattern of life remains unchanged. In reality, this may not be the case. In the first place, much will depend on the technology involved. With *renovation,* it is often possible for a family to remain in the dwelling but although empirical evidence is not at hand, there can be little doubt about the disruptive effect of 'having the builders in' for weeks on end and seeing the home torn apart. *Wreckout* obviously requires households being moved, usually to vacant accommodation in the same area. Frequently this accommodation is only temporary and households move back to their former homes when renovation is complete. Even so, the disruptive effect can be considerable, particularly when households are moved into furnished accommodation and separated from the majority of their possessions and household effects. As with relocation, stress is frequently heightened by uncertainty and delay. Rarely are authorities able to predict the date when the work will begin and end and many households seem to find the waiting period particularly stressful.

If these were the only effects of rehabilitation, perhaps it might be correct to argue that the process is less disruptive than clearance. It is unusual for the community to remain intact, however. Rarely are all of the households able to return to their former accommodation or, even, to remain in the same locality. There are several reasons for this. In the first place, families living in overcrowded conditions are usually rehoused in more suitable accommodation, while in certain cases households have to move to alternative locations because the rehabilitation programme has involved a reduction in the number of dwelling units. What is more, there is evidence to suggest that even if relocation is avoided during the rehabilitation process, the subsequent increase in rent not only causes material hardship but also forces many households out of their refurbished homes. For instance, in America, Warren (1965) reports that in a survey of forty municipalities with rehabilitation programmes, almost half claimed that many of the original residents were forced to move. As a result of rehabilitation, many essentially working-class areas were being invaded by upper income groups. This process, known as gentrification, is not confined to America and is well documented in the Shelter publication *Home Improvements, People or Profit?* (Pearson and Henney, 1972). This reveals that in many areas in Britain, rents have risen far beyond the reach of the original tenants as a result of rehabilitation and large profits have been made. The report cites the example of rents for furnished accommodation in one London borough increasing from an average of £5.70 before improvement to £22.39 after. The example may be extreme but it demonstrates both the gentrification process and the profits that can be made out of the rehabilitation programme. Further evidence of the abuse of rehabilitation is provided by the National Community Development Project in its 1975 publication *The Poverty of the Improvement Programme.* Here the case of the Glowshire Property Co. is outlined. The company is said to have purchased tenanted or vacant housing in Saltby (Birmingham) and used its own building firm to renovate the properties with the aid of Government subsidies. Subsequently the properties were sold through the company's estate agency using finance provided by the company's mortgage business. The report suggests that mortgage interest rates were in the order of 25 per cent and gives an example of one property being bought for £1 400 and resold, after modernisation, for £3 250. On the basis of this evidence, it would seem that in certain circumstances established communities have been broken up by rehabilitation and the urban poor have not necessarily benefited from the programme. Certainly it is not inconceivable that, without rigorous checks and controls, any private-sector rehabilitation programme could be abused in this way.

In those cases where the property is refurbished for occupation by the lower income groups, a further criticism frequently focuses on the quality of the accommodation. For instance, Needleman (1965, p. 200) points out that 'the quality of accommodation provided by the rehabilitated house will not be so high as that given by the completely new house' and the director of Housing for the London County Council finds 'that tenants, on the whole, prefer new accommodation to the rehabilitated dwellings' (Allerton, 1963, p. 252). Evidence from America tends to support this assertion. From an examination of the rental–sale housing market in Philadelphia, Bagby (1973, p. 55) concludes that 'the policy to provide rehabilitated housing to low income residents represents – in their eyes at least – a conscious decision to furnish them with a lower quality residence than would be provided by a new dwelling.' Similarly, Listokin (1973, p. 10) points out that in New York 'even after an expenditure of $26 400 per unit, the rehabilitated old-law tenements still had serious deficiencies such as a lack of light, air, privacy and acoustical control.' What is more, very few rehabilitation programmes bring about any improvement in the quality of the residential environment. Even in the public sector in Britain, relatively little attention is paid to environmental improvements. The National Community Development Project (1975, p. 9) points out, for instance, that 'compared with redeveloped areas, even those General Improvement Areas where environmental work has been done have fared badly. There is no money for community facilities.' As one American contractor has observed 'one of the problems (of rehabilitation) is that you're not creating an environment that anyone wants to live in . . . no playgrounds, poorly lit streets, bad schools. . . .' (Bagby, 1973, p. 56.) Given the evidence on gentrification and rents outlined earlier, this may be something of an overstatement, but it would certainly appear that the social implications of rehabilitation need not necessarily be of benefit to the urban poor, nor need they be superior to those of redevelopment and clearance.

ECONOMIC ASPECTS

One of the major arguments in favour of rehabilitation is that it is quicker and cheaper than clearance and rehousing, but, there are considerable differences of opinion as to whether this is the case and the evidence is often conflicting. Since there is relatively little empirical evidence and circumstances differ from one geographical location to another as a result of differences in such varied factors as the skill and expertise of the local builders, building costs, weather conditions, etc. it is difficult to arrive at a definite conclusion. In America, evidence from the Boston Rehabilitation Programme indicates that approximately 2 000 dwellings were rehabilitated in less than a year, 'whereas the demolition of 2 000 existing units and their replacement would have taken twice as long' (Listokin, 1973, p. 122). By comparison, the National Community Development Project (1975, p. 12) concludes that in Britain the 'improvement policy has often proved slower than redevelopment . . . It has been cheaper, primarily because it is cheaper to improve a few houses than to redevelop the whole area.' Bagby (1973) reaches a similar conclusion over costs in his comparative study of rehabilitation, new construction and urban renewal costs in Philadelphia. He concludes that total rehabilitation is 12 per cent cheaper than new construction and between 22 and 24 per cent cheaper than clearance and new construction. Although Bagby's findings relate to a particular neighbourhood in Philadelphia at a particular point in time, his conclusion that rehabilitation is less expensive than new construction seems to find support elsewhere in the United States. Listokin (1973) points out that in 1971, the Housing and Urban Development estimate of the average construction costs for new low-rent public housing was $17 900, whereas the average cost of rehabilitation was only $8 170. A smaller, but similar, differential was found in Chicago where the unit cost of rehabilitation ($10 000) compared favourably with the unit cost of new construction ($15 000). In Boston, rehabilitation costs per project were found to range from $48 000 to $165 000 whereas new construction was estimated at between $51 000 and $199 000 per project.

It would seem, therefore, that rehabilitation is cheaper than clearance and rehousing, but, although it is cheaper, rehabilitation need not be more economic. In *The Economics of Housing*, Needleman (1965, p. 201) points out that the comparative economics of rehabilitation and reconstruction depend on the rate of interest, the future life of the renovated property and the difference between the running of new and renovated property. Needleman argues that 'the higher the rate of interest, the longer the life of the improved accommodation and the smaller the difference between the annual running costs of the two categories of dwelling, the greater the advantage of modernisation over building anew.' He suggests, therefore, that rehabilitation is worthwhile if the present cost of rebuilding exceeds the cost of modernisation plus the present value of the cost of rebuilding, plus the present value of the difference in annual running costs. Algebraically this takes the form:

$$b > m + b(1 + i)^{-\lambda} + \frac{r}{i}(1 - (1 + i)^{-\lambda})$$

where m = the cost of adequate modernisation
  b = the cost of demolition and rebuilding
  i = the interest rate
  λ = the useful life of the modernised property in years
  r = the difference in annual repair costs

$b(1 + i)^{-\lambda}$ = the present value of b in λ years' time at a rate of interest, i

$\frac{r}{i}(1 - (1 + i)^{-\lambda})$ = the present value of r annually for λ years at a rate of interest, i.

Needleman's formula has been criticised by several authors. Sigsworth and Wilkinson (1967), for instance, suggest that the capital value of the house before improvement should be added to the right-hand side of the equation so that the formula reads:

$$b > m + c + b(1 + i)^{-\lambda} + \frac{r}{i}(1 - (1 + i)^{-\lambda})$$

where c = the capital value of the house before improvement.

In his reply to this criticism, Needleman (1968, p. 88) argues that the value of the house before improvement 'has no relevance to the choice between modernisation and improvement' and points out that although his original formula deals with only five factors, it can be modified easily. For instance, Needleman claims that if, as Sigsworth and Wilkinson suggest, replacement costs might be expected to rise in the future, the formula can be adjusted to take account of this and the decision rule would become, modernise if:

$$b > m + b\left(\frac{1 + z}{1 + i}\right)\lambda + \frac{r}{i}(1 - (1 + i)^{-\lambda})$$

where z = the expected annual rate of increase in replacement costs.

A further, perhaps more fundamental and positive criticism of Needleman's original formula is made by Schaaf (1969, p. 401) who claims that it 'contains one error and, more importantly, ignores a number of complicating factors'. Schaaf uses the following version of the Needleman formula for his analysis:

$$C > \left(R + M\frac{1 - (1 + i)^{-n}}{i} + \frac{C}{(1 + i)n}\right)$$

where C = new construction
R = rehabilitation cost
M = annual saving in maintenance costs with a new structure rather than a rehabilitated one
n = life of present structure following rehabilitation
i = discount rate.

He argues that the error concerns the term $C/(1 + i)n$ which is used to measure the present value of the amount required to replace a structure when the effects of rehabilitation are no longer evident. He suggests that it is incorrect to assume that there would be no difference between rehabilitation and replacement if $C = (R + C/(1 + i)n)$ since a property owner would have a structure n years old in n years if he replaces, whereas if he rehabilitates and invests $C/1 + i)$ he will have an amount equal to the cost of a new structure in n years. According to Schaaf, therefore, the correct relationship is

$$C = (R + C(1 - nr)/(1 + i)n)$$

where r is the annual depreciation rate of the new structure.

While this revision appears to correct the error in the formula, Schaaf points to the various shortcomings of the original work. He argues that Needleman's original formula ignores the fact that different standards of rehabilitation and new construction are possible and that the formula does not consider the fact that a new structure may provide a higher level of amenity than a rehabilitated unit or, in certain cases, vice versa. He suggests that this problem could be resolved by using rent differences as an index of the differences in amenity and advocates that the formula should be further modified to include a term (D) which represents the difference in the annual rental income of a new structure and a rehabilitated structure. His modified formula suggests that rehabilitation is feasible for any standard if:

$$C > \left(R + M\frac{1 - (1+i)^{-n}}{i} + \frac{C(1-nr)}{(1+i)^n} + D\frac{1-(1+i)^{-n}}{i}\right)$$

and the optimum level or rehabilitation is the one that optimises Y when

$$Y = C - \left(R + M\frac{1 - (1+i)^{-n}}{i} + \frac{C(1-nr)}{(1+i)^n} + D\frac{1-(1+i)^{-n}}{i}\right)$$

Having made these amendments, Schaaf recognises that further modifications would be necessary before this basic model could be used in all possible circumstances and suggests that three types of changes and additions are necessary. First, he suggests that it is necessary to identify the length of life and corresponding depreciation rate associated with each renewal standard; second, to limit all investment situations to a period equal to the length of life of the new structures; third, to take account of differences in future rehabilitation investment. To demonstrate the method of incorporating these changes in the basic model he investigates the feasibility of rehabilitating a structure to *code compliance* on three occasions and then to the *modernisation* standard. He points out that the feasibility analysis of this situation requires that the following formula is resolved:

$$C - \left[R_1 + \frac{R_1}{(1+i)^{n_1}} + \frac{R_1}{(1+i)^{2n_1}} + \frac{R_3(r_3(n_c - 3n_1))}{(1+i)^{3n_1}} \right.$$
$$+ M_1 \frac{1 - (1+i)^{-3n_1}}{i} + D_1 \frac{1 - (1+i)^{-3n_1}}{i}$$
$$\left. + M_3 \frac{\dfrac{1 - (1+i)^{-(n_c - 3n_1)}}{i}}{(1+i)^{3_1}} + D_3 \frac{\dfrac{1 - (1+i)^{-(n_c - 3n_1)}}{i}}{(1+i)^{3n_1}} \right]$$

where
- R_1 = cost of code compliance
- R_3 = cost of modernisation
- C = cost of new construction
- n_1 = Life of structure rehabilitated to the code compliance standard
- n_3 = life of structure rehabilitated to the modernization standard,

$$r_3 = \frac{100}{n_3} \text{ per cent,}$$

- n_c = life of new structure
- M_1 = difference in maintenance costs between a new structure and one rehabilitated to the code compliance standard
- D_1 = difference in rent levels between a new structure and one rehabilitated to the code compliance standard
- M_3 = difference in maintenance costs between a new structure and one rehabilitated to the modernisation standard, and
- D_3 = difference in rent levels between a new structure and one rehabilitated to the modernisation standard.

If, as in Schaaf's worked example of this situation, the total cost of rehabilitation exceeds the cost of immediate new construction, the particular pattern of rehabilitation investment is not feasible.

Undoubtedly Schaaf's modifications have brought greater accuracy and sophistication to the original formula but for many practising planners, the calibration of the formula for the various renewal possibilities may be somewhat time-consuming and, perhaps, unwieldy. Accordingly, several less-sophisticated methods have been devised in an attempt to determine the most appropriate renewal strategy. Lean (1971) outlines two – the rate of return and capital value methods. With the former, the property is seen as an investment and the objective is to determine which strategy will yield the greatest income over time. In order to emphasise the essential principles, Lean makes several qualifying assumptions – that no tax has to be paid on income from investment and sinking fund earnings, that there is no difference between rehabilitation and redevelopment in terms of disturbance costs and that there are no earnings on the differences in cost between redevelopment and rehabilitation. Lean goes on to suggest that, as a result of these assumptions, it is possible to calculate the rate of return on the various policies from

$$r = \frac{nr - sf}{c} \times 100$$

where
r = rate of return

c = cost of rehabilitation or redevelopment (including cost of improvement to the environment)

nr = increase in net rent

sf = amount annually that will accumulate to c at 5 per cent compound for the term of years.

Lean recognises that it might be difficult, in many areas, to make realistic calculations of market rents and that it is often easier to obtain evidence of capital values. Where this is the case, he suggests that an economic assessment can be made by making 'a comparison between the costs of rehabilitation and the difference in capital values before and after the rehabilitation and the costs of redevelopment and the differences in capital values before and after the redevelopment' (Lean, 1971, p. 228). As an example, Lean cites a hypothetical case where £3 000 spent on redevelopment increases unit values by £3 300, whereas £1 000 spent on rehabilitation might increase values by £1 500. In this case, redevelopment would not be worthwhile since £3 000 spent on rehabilitation would increase values by £4 500.

A completely different approach is outlined by Isaacson (1976) in his paper 'Choosing renewal options'. Developed jointly by the Department of the Environment and the London Borough of Southwark, the methodology is intended to 'afford a reasonably quick and simple method for assessing the problems (of residential areas) and proposing solutions to them' (Isaacson, 1976, p. 11). The method involves identifying the main house-types in an area, designing a range of likely improvements, evaluating the quality of the property and its environment and assigning values to these qualities to determine the improvement potential. The two sets of values for environmental and dwelling improvement potential can be combined to give a single value which is then used to decide the amount worth spending on rehabilitation. Alternatively, dwellings in an area can be classified according to three quality groups – poor, medium and good. The same can be done for the environment and these categories can then be combined in a matrix to give nine dwelling/environment groups. These groups can be placed in rank order from best to worst and likely renewal options can be linked to each. It should not be difficult to pick out likely combinations since there are only nine basic classes of accommodation and six basic options (redevelopment, selective clearance, infill development, improvement and conversion, maintenance and repair, doing nothing).

CONCLUSION

The factors influencing rehabilitation/redevelopment are so varied that it is impossible to state categorically that rehabilitation is more or less economic than redevelopment. Each project has to be examined individually using one of the many appraisal methods. Few, if any, of these seem to take account of the non-economic factors which have to be considered when evaluating the advantages and disadvantages of rehabilitation over clearance and redevelopment. Indeed the sociological advantages of rehabilitation over redevelopment seem to be more apparent in theory than in practice, and it would appear that if rehabilitation is to be socially beneficial to the lower income groups, programmes must be carefully controlled and monitored. Rehabilitation can help to raise the quality of the housing stock. Carefully administered it can also help improve the living conditions of the urban poor and, at the same time, can have a less disruptive effect than clearance and redevelopment on both the community and the individual household. While confined to the rehabilitation of dwellings and, to a lesser extent, the residential environment, it can do little, however, to ameliorate the social problems of slums. This requires the rehabilitation of people.

SECTION 2
RESIDENTIAL RENEWAL
IN BRITAIN

As outlined in the Introduction, the aim of this section is to provide a case illustration of some of the major conclusions derived from Section 1. By examining the British approach, it is possible to demonstrate several points. These include the effect of subjectivity on the identification of slum properties, the role of obsolescence and rising standards on the formation of slums and the reasons for the failure of the housing programme to eliminate the slum problem. To do this, the study examines, first, the scale of the problem and then goes on to review the response of successive British Governments and the effectiveness of Government policy.

CHAPTER 7
THE SLUM PROBLEM
IN BRITAIN

Although the problem of slum housing had been recognised officially in Britain in the nineteenth century, it was not until the 1930s that the modern slum clearance programme was evolved formally. Under Section 25 of the Housing Act of 1930, every local authority with a population of more than 20 000 was instructed to produce a general statement of its plans for dealing with slum clearance. 'The programmes then put forward by 145 local authorities . . . provided for clearing 76 524 houses.' (Ministry of Health, 1934, p. 2.) Over the next three years, the Government came to the conclusion that the rate at which slums were being dealt with was too slow and in the *Ministry of Health Circular to Housing Authorities, 1331,* issued on 6 April 1933, all of the authorities in England and Wales were instructed to submit, not later than 30 September 1933, complete programmes for the abolition of slums within five years. In response, the programmes put forward by the original 145 local authorities rose from 76 524 to 172 261 in three years and the magnitude of the country's slum problem was officially placed at 266 851 dwellings. By 1937, the programmes had been further increased to 377 930 and in 1939, the Ministry of Health reported that 'further reviews by the local authorities revealed more houses which can only be dealt with satisfactorily by demolition' (Ministry of Health, 1939, p. 81). Accordingly, the figure was raised to 472 000. With the advent of the Second World War and the post-war housing shortage, the next official estimate did not take place until 1954. Once again, local authorities were required, under Section 1 of the Housing Repairs and Rents Act of 1954, to submit proposals for dealing with their slums. They reported (Ministry of Housing and Local Government, 1955) that some 847 112 dwellings were unfit and that some 375 484 should be demolished within five years, while 88 278 could be retained for temporary accommodation. Apparently, the magnitude of the slum problem had almost doubled over the fifteen years between 1939 and 1954.

By 1960, the situation appeared to have worsened still further since Gray and Russell (1962) concluded from their survey of the housing situation in England and Wales that there were 622 000 unfit accommodation units, plus 210 000 with an estimated life of less than five years and a further 1 122 000 with a life of less than fifteen years. Some improvement seemed to have occurred by 1964, however, as the Government Housing Survey reported that '515 000 accommodation units were estimated to be unfit at the end of 1964 and a further 218 000 to have a life of less that five years; that is, barring any radical improvement to these dwellings, 733 000 would need to be replaced within the five years 1964–69.' (Woolf, 1967, p. 95.) The returns made to the Ministry of Housing during 1965, in response to Circular No. 11/65, revealed that the local authorities themselves considered that there were 824 000 dwellings which were unfit by the current standard (Central Housing Advisory Committee, 1966). Not believing the accuracy of these figures, the Minister for Housing initiated a further, independent inquiry in 1967. The survey, carried out by public health inspectors seconded to the Ministry of Housing, revealed that 'there were more unfit houses and more substandard houses than had been known before, and they were not so concentrated as had been believed before, but more spread out.' (Ministry of Housing and Local Government, 1968a, p. 1.) The results indicated that, far from being under 1 million as the 1965 survey had suggested, the number of unfit dwellings was in the order of 1.836 million. Four years later, however, in 1971, the number of unfit dwellings was revealed to have declined quite markedly. A new house condition survey, based on the sample used in 1967, revealed that the number of unfit dwellings had apparently fallen from over 1.8 million to 1.244 million (Department of the Environment, 1973a). This represented a reduction of approximately 600 000 dwellings or almost 33 per cent in only four years. Even so, after more than forty years of attempting to eliminate slum housing, the British Government appears to be faced with a slum problem in England and Wales which is approximately five times greater than was suggested by the first comprehensive estimates in 1933. To explain this development, it is necessary to examine several factors, including the accuracy of the estimates, the nature of the standards and the achievements of the slum clearance programmes.

THE ACCURACY OF THE STATISTICS

As the previous section has indicated, the official figures are, in fact, estimates of the magnitude of the slum problem in England and Wales. What is more, they are estimates based on two different sources. The figures for 1933, 1954 and 1965 were based on the estimates by individual local authorities of the number of unfit dwellings in their areas, whereas the 1960, 1964, 1967 and 1971 figures were derived from independent sample surveys. Clearly, while the two sets of figures might be expected to produce results which are broadly comparable, there is no reason why they should coincide exactly, since the nature of the errors involved in the estimating procedures is different. While the former should, in theory at least, provide estimates based on a complete coverage of the slum problem, the latter provide estimates based on sample surveys. Quite clearly, the results of a survey based on a sample do not necessarily coincide exactly with the results derived from a full-scale study of the total population. Still further discrepancies between the two sets of figures might be expected as a result of the survey procedure, since the views of local government employees are more likely to be influenced by local conditions and the policies of their employers, than are those of independent investigators.

Since the two sets of estimates are derived from different sources and might be expected to contain different types of error, perhaps it is best to examine their accuracy separately.

LOCAL AUTHORITY ESTIMATES

In *Our Older Homes: a Call for Action,* the Dennington Committee makes the rather curious observation on the 1965 local authority estimates that 'although there are doubts about the accuracy of some of the individual returns, the totals show the magnitude of the task of dealing with the nation's unfit houses . . .' (Central Housing Advisory Committee, 1966, p. 8). Presumably this infers that some authorities have overestimated, while others have underestimated the extent of the slum problem in their areas – the errors cancel out and the returns are an accurate estimate of the overall size of the slum problem. However, the statement is curious for several reasons. First, it goes on to point out that the totals show that the bulk of the nation's unfit houses 'are concentrated in relatively few areas' (Central Housing Advisory Committee, 1966, p. 8). This seems to be a somewhat surprising conclusion given the admission that there are doubts about the accuracy of the individual returns. Second, it is difficult to see how the totals can be seen as an indication of the magnitude of the problem without evidence to show that the errors cancel out. Third, it is curious, perhaps, that errors should exist at all. In *Old Houses into New Homes*, the Ministry of Housing and Local Government (1968a, p. 1) elaborates on this question of error in local authority returns. It points out 'that some of these estimates were rather rough and different authorities naturally applied different standards'. Indeed, these are the two major criticisms; the estimates lack both standardisation and objectivity. In the 1954 estimates, for instance, it would appear that certain authorities included all unfit houses in their figures while others reduced the numbers to manageable proportions and yet others may deliberately have ignored certain properties for fear of the image that the authority might acquire. Thus the note accompanying the 1954 statistics warned that the estimates only 'represent the best conclusions which local authorities have been able to reach in the light of their local circumstances. There is, however, considerable variation in the information on which they are based: some local authorities have been able to carry out a detailed inspection whereas some have had to rely on broad estimates.' (Ministry of Housing and Local Government, 1955, p. iii.) What is more, the statistics are rarely complete. For instance, the 1933 returns exclude the programmes of 288 authorities, while the 1954 proposals of thirty-two authorities were not received in time for publication in the 1955 report. This is a point which is frequently overlooked. Even so, it is generally accepted that the local authority figures underestimate the magnitude of the slum problem in England and Wales.

INDEPENDENT ESTIMATES

The four independent surveys have provided data on the residential rateable unit – the separately rated hereditament listed in the valuation records. For these surveys, information was derived from three sources – questionnaire surveys of the households occupying a sample of the rateable units in England and Wales to determine the standard of accommodation and household characteristics; information from the local authority on the fitness and estimated life of the rateable units in the sample and, where necessary, information on the tenure of the rateable units from the Inland Revenue. As mentioned previously, public health inspectors were employed to undertake the surveys. Each had considerable experience in assessing the structural conditions of houses but certain precautions were taken to avoid bias, particularly in the 1967 and 1971 surveys. No inspector was allocated an area within 50 miles of his home and each had to survey ten completely different areas outside London. In addition, careful checks were carried out before and during the fieldwork to ensure that observer errors were kept to a minimum.

In each case, a sample size of about 6 000 units was considered to be sufficient to give reasonably accurate national estimates. In 1960, the occupants of 3 003 rateable units were interviewed in Greater London and 3 002 elsewhere in England and Wales. The sample was drawn from the valuation lists held by the local valuation office of the

Inland Revenue. In Greater London, every 800th rateable unit was selected but outside Greater London, a different sampling fraction was used and two strata were formed – the fourteen largest towns forming one and the remainder of England and Wales the other. Details of the sampling procedure are provided in Gray and Russell (1962). The same sample was used in 1964 but an allowance was made for new units entering the population and certain households in Greater London were not interviewed because they had been reinterviewed in 1963 to provide data for the Milner–Holland Committee. For these units, either the 1963 data on the availability of amenities or changes in the state of the property since 1960 were used, or information was obtained from the local authority. This procedure resulted in a total sample of 3 101 rateable units in Greater London and 3 250 in the rest of England and Wales.

In 1967 and 1971, a slightly different sampling procedure was adopted although the valuation lists were used as the sampling frame once more, the rateable unit was the sample unit and the country was divided into Greater London and the rest of England and Wales. The sampling procedure adopted in 1967 is outlined in the Ministry of Housing and Local Government report on the survey which was published in May 1968 edition *Economic Trends*. Suffice it to point out that overall, the 1967 survey was based on the inspection of 6 044 rateable units. The 1971 survey utilised the same sample with an allowance for new building giving an intended sample size of 6 215 units. The effective sample was much less than this, at 5 813 units, largely as a result of demolitions and the exclusion of units no longer considered to be dwellings. In the report on the survey, however, the investigators make the rather strange observation that 'in a few cases where addresses were not traced by surveyors, it is believed that the units had not been demolished.' (Department of the Environment, 1973a, p. 2.) Even so, it is clear that in the various independent surveys, efforts were made to avoid bias and to select a sample which was representative of the overall housing situation in the country. Each of the surveys recognised that the results were only estimates and gave some indication of the reliability of the figures. In the 1964 and 1967 surveys, for instance, the approximate standard errors of the estimate were as follows:

ESTIMATE	APPROXIMATE STANDARD ERROR	
(no. of rateable units)	1964 survey	1967 survey
100 000	31 000	40 000
250 000	49 000	65 000
500 000	67 000	90 000
1 000 000	92 000	125 000
2 000 000	122 000	170 000

Source: Woolf (1967) and Ministry of Housing and Local Government (1968b).

Despite these attempts to eliminate bias and increase objectivity, doubts about the accuracy of the estimates remain. Speaking in the House of Commons on 27 November 1972, Mr R. Freeson (Member for Willesden, East) said that, given the developments in the country since 1967, he could not accept the 1971 slum figure as accurate and suggested that there had been some mistake. In his reply, Mr P. Channon (The Minister for Housing and Construction) conceded that 'it is just possible, I suppose, that the 1967 figure was wrong' (House of Commons, 1972, col. 164). Perhaps the allegations carry certain political overtones but, on the evidence available, it would seem that one or both of the surveys entailed a margin of inaccuracy which was in excess of the anticipated margins of error.

THE NATURE OF THE STANDARDS

In Chapter 2, it was pointed out that in Britain, interpretation of the official standard for determining whether a dwelling is suitable for continued habitation is highly subjective. As was pointed out at the time, this subjectivity of interpretation is, in some respects, one of the strengths of the British legislation, but in others it is one of its major weaknesses. The principal weakness is associated with the fact that the standard can be applied differently in different parts of the country and at different periods in time, thereby resulting in the sort of discrepancies referred to above. In recent years, efforts have been made to introduce greater objectivity but in the early years the standards were even more vague than they are at present. Although the 1930 Housing Act can be regarded as the basis of the modern slum clearance programme, it did not lay down any precise standards of fitness for human habitation. In the first place it instructed that 'where a local authority, upon consideration of an official representation, or a report from any of its officers, or other information in its possession, is satisfied that any dwelling-house . . . is in any respect unfit for human habitation . . .' (Housing Act, 1930, Section 17(1)), it could require that the accommodation be demolished or, where appropriate, rendered fit for habitation under Section 62(3). It went on to advise that 'in determining . . . whether a house is fit for human habitation regard shall be had to the extent, if any, to which by reason of disrepair or sanitary defects the house falls short of the provisions of any by-laws in operation in the district. . . .' However, it did define sanitary defects as 'lack of air space or of ventilation, darkness, dampness, absence of adequate and readily accessible water supply or sanitary accommodation or of other conveniences and inadequate paving or drainage of courts, yards or passages' (Housing Act, 1930, Section 62(1)).

Clearly, the standards were open to a variety of interpretations. Not only would local by-laws vary from one locality to another, but so would views as to what conditions could be regarded as being 'adequate','inadequate' or 'readily accessible'. Despite this, the definition was incorporated in the Housing Act of 1936 but in 1946, the lack of precision was recognised by the Central Housing Advisory Committee Sub-Committee on Standards of Fitness for Habitation. The Sub-Committee recommended that the fitness consideration outlined in Section 188 of the Housing Act, 1936, should be replaced by a minimum fitness standard prescribed by law. The standard recommended was, in fact, a standard which the Ministry of Health had outlined in 1919 in its *Manual of Unfit Houses*. This suggested that a fit house should be free from serious damp, satisfactorily lighted and ventilated, properly drained and provided with adequate sanitary conveniences and with a sink and suitable arrangements for the disposal of slop water and should be in good general repair. In addition, the manual further recommended that the house should possess a satisfactory water supply, adequate washing accommodation, adequate facilities for preparing and cooking food and a well-ventilated food store. These recommendations, though still maintaining a high degree of subjectivity, were incorporated into Government legislation under Section 9 of the Housing Repairs and Rents Act, 1954, and, as outlined in Chapter 2, form the basis of Section 4(1) of the Housing Act, 1957. When the second major review of slum housing was undertaken in 1954, local authorities were required to estimate the 'number of houses unfit for human habitation within the meaning of Section 9 of the Housing Repairs and Rents Act, 1954' (Ministry of Housing and Local Government, 1954, p. 17). Clearly both the estimating procedure and the subjectivity of the standard left considerable scope for error.

In addition to recommending a minimum fitness standard, the sub-committee suggested a standard for a satisfactory house. This became the basis for the improvement grant standard introduced under the Housing Act, 1949, and is used for administering the system of discretionary improvement grants. As was pointed out in the previous chapter, this has become known as the 'twelve point' standard. It provides that a dwelling must:

(i) be in a good state of repair and substantially free from damp;
(ii) have each room properly lighted and ventilated;
(iii) have an adequate supply of wholesome water laid on inside the dwelling;
(iv) be provided with efficient and adequate means of supplying hot water for domestic purposes;
(v) have an internal water closet, if practicable, otherwise a readily accessible outside water closet;
(vi) have a fixed bath or shower in a bathroom;
(vii) be provided with a sink or sinks, and with suitable arrangements for the disposal of waste water;
(viii) have a proper drainage system;
(ix) be provided in each room with adequate points for gas or electric lighting (where reasonably available);
(x) be provided with adequate facilities for heating;
(vi) have satisfactory facilities for storing, preparing and cooking food;
(xii) have proper provision for storing fuel (where required).

While focusing on the features that ought to be taken into consideration in assessing housing fitness, this standard, like its predecessors, clearly contained a high degree of subjectivity. Not until 1959 was an absolute, objective standard introduced. The House Purchase and Housing Act of 1959 laid down five standard amenities with which every fit dwelling should be equipped: a fixed bath or shower in a bathroom, a wash-hand basin, hot water supply, a water closet in or contiguous to the dwelling and a food store. If a dwelling did not possess one or more of these amenities it was unfit and the owner was entitled to a grant towards the cost of bringing the dwelling up to standard. Since 1959, the standard has been modified on several occasions. Section 30(3) of the Housing Act, 1961, laid down that the water closet need not necessarily be in or attached to the dwelling, while Section 43(2) of the Housing Act, 1964, stated that the fixed bath or shower need not necessarily be in a separate bathroom and Section 49 of the 1964 Act also amended the provision regarding the water supply. By 1964, therefore, the standard had been so modified that a fit house was equipped with a fixed bath or shower, a wash-hand basin, a hot and cold water supply at a fixed bath or shower, wash-hand basin and sink, a water closet and a ventilated food store. Under the 1969 Housing Act, the standard was further modified, as has already been pointed out, to exclude the ventilated food store.

These new, more objective, standards have become the basis for the more recent estimates of housing fitness. The 1960 survey, for instance, measured fitness on the basis of the five standard amenities of the House Purchase and Housing Act, 1959. By 1964, the standards had been modified, as outlined above, and the standard used on this occasion was the modified version. In addition, the 1964 survey required the local authorities to indicate 'whether each rateable unit in the sample was

(a) included in the total of unfit houses submitted in the returns made to the Ministry of Housing and Local Government under Section 1 of the Housing Repairs and Rents Act, 1954, or in proposals under Section 2 of the Housing Act, 1957;
(b) the subject of an official representation, on a report from any of the Council's officers as unfit under the Housing Act, 1957.' (Woolf, 1967, p. 70.)

By comparison, the 1967 survey assessed whether the unit was unfit by the criteria of Section 4(1) of the Housing Act, 1957, and whether the occupants had exclusive use of a fixed bath or shower, a wash-hand basin, a hot and cold water supply to a bath, wash-hand basin and kitchen sink, and a water closet inside the dwelling (Ministry of Housing and Local Government, 1968b, p. xxiv). The same criteria were adopted in 1971, but the survey collected information on the exclusive use of five amenities, rather than the four utilised in 1967. In 1971, data were collected on the four amenities identified in the 1967 survey, plus the presence or absence of a sink.

CONCLUSION

Despite forty years of slum clearance, the slum problem in England and Wales appears to be considerably larger than it was when its extent was first comprehensively measured in 1933. Part of the explanation for this phenomenon must be that the early local authority returns tended to underestimate the magnitude of the problem. In recent years, more objective standards have been introduced and the degree of subjective judgement in the estimates has been reduced. However, the standards employed tend to vary from survey to survey and it is not always possible to measure the effectiveness of slum elimination programmes from the results of such surveys. As living standards rise and the worst of the housing conditions are eliminated, so the minimum acceptable fitness level is also raised. This point was made in Chapter 3, where it was stressed that the problem of slum housing is an on-going process. Only recently has the point been appreciated fully in Britain. In 1933, the intention was to secure the demolition of all slum houses by 1938 and this sort of objective has been repeated on numerous occasions since. Even in November 1972, Mr P. Channon (the Minister for Housing and Construction) was noting that earlier in the year his predecessor had invited local authorities to 'join a drive to ensure that within ten years, no one was required to live in an unfit or substandard house' (House of Commons, 1972, col. 159). By the time the slum houses of 1972 have been cleared, however, the minimum acceptable fitness standard will be such that many further properties will be classified as unsuitable for continued occupation. Much depends on the level at which the standard is set. If it is too low, the slum problem can disappear virtually over night. Conversely, if it is set unrealistically high, slum eradication policies can appear to be having little, if any, impact on the problem. To determine the success of the various slum eradication programmes, it is necessary to examine the actual programmes. This will be undertaken in Chapters 8 and 9 but, in the meantime, it is important to stress that, despite the inaccuracy of the estimates, it is clear that the magnitude of the problem was not, and is not, uniform throughout the country. As Bowley (1945, p. 155) has observed the bulk of the slums were found, in 1933, to be concentrated in the older industrial towns and London. Over one-third of the houses to be demolished in 1933 were situated in London, Birmingham, Leeds, Liverpool and Manchester (Table 7.1). By 1954, the same five towns accounted for less than one-fifth of the total number of unfit properties and it would appear that either the 'big five' (as they had become known) had done much to reduce their problems or conditions had worsened in the other areas. It has to be appreciated, however, that the two sets of statistics are not directly comparable. Apart from the lack of standardisation referred to above, it should be remembered that the 1933 returns did not include the programmes for 288 authorities, whereas only 32 authorities failed to submit proposals in 1954.

In 1962 Burnett and Scott's survey of housing conditions in England and Wales stressed the variable nature of the housing problem. The analysis identified ten areas, mainly in the conurbations, where the incidence and volume of substandard housing

Table 7.1 Size of slum clearance programmes for selected towns in England and Wales, 1933 and 1954 compared

	HOUSES TO BE DEMOLISHED AS PERCENTAGE OF ENGLAND AND WALES TOTAL	
	1933	1954
London	12.4	8.5
Birmingham	1.7	1.6
Leeds	11.2	3.8
Liverpool	4.5	1.9
Manchester	5.6	2.0
Total	35.4	17.8

Source: Ministry of Health (1934) and Ministry of Housing and Local Government (1955).

was greatest. It was concluded that the areas with the highest proportions of substandard dwellings were 'West Yorkshire and the contiguous parts of South East Lancashire and North East Cheshire and the Durham coalfield. Next in order would appear to be South Wales and Tyneside . . . Liverpool and Bootle also stand high on the list.' (Burnett and Scott, 1962, p. 77). What the study revealed, therefore, was that the problem was most severe in the urban regions centred on Leeds, Manchester, Cardiff, Newcastle and Liverpool.

As was pointed out earlier, the results of the 1967 housing survey indicated that unfit housing was more widespread than had been believed. Certainly the problem did not appear to be as severe in the country's six major conurbations (Tyneside, West Yorkshire, South East Lancashire, Merseyside, West Midlands and Greater London) or in the other urban areas (Table 7.2). Rather, it was in the rural districts that conditions appeared to be most chronic. Whereas the conurbations accounted for 33.9 per cent of the total dwelling stock in England and Wales, they possessed no more than 32.7 per cent of the country's unfit housing and only 11.3 per cent of the dwellings in the

Table 7.2 Unfit dwellings in England and Wales by type of area, 1967 and 1971 compared

	ALL DWELLINGS		UNFIT DWELLINGS			
			As % of total for England and Wales		As % of total for each area	
	%	%				
	1967	1971	1967	1971	1967	1971
Conurbation	33.9	32.6	32.7	36.2	11.3	8.1
Other urban areas	45.6	45.9	43.9	43.3	11.3	6.9
Rural districts	20.5	21.5	23.4	20.5	13.3	6.9

Source: Ministry of Housing and Local Government (1968b, p. xxxi) and Department of the Environment (1973a, p. 12).

conurbations were unfit for habitation. A similar situation appeared to exist in the other urban areas of the country. Although 45.6 per cent of the country's housing was found in these areas, only 11.3 per cent of it was unfit for occupation and these unfit properties accounted for no more that 43.9 per cent of the total unfit property in England and Wales. In the rural areas, however, slightly more than 13 per cent of the property was found to be unfit and whereas the rural districts accounted for 20.5 per cent of the total dwelling stock, some 23.4 per cent of the country's unfit dwellings were found here. On the basis of these figures, therefore, it would appear that in 1967, the problem of unfit housing was greatest in the rural areas. By 1971, however, the situation appeared to have changed quite considerably and it was in the main urban areas, once more, that the problem was most severe. From Table 7.2, it would appear that the rate of improvement in the conurbations over the four-year period, 1967–71, had been considerably lower than in the rural districts and 'other' urban areas with the result that approximately 36 per cent of the country's unfit homes were to be found in the conurbations, although these areas accounted for no more than one-third of the total dwelling stock.

Since four of the country's six major conurbations are to be found in the old industrial areas of the North of England, perhaps it is not surprising to find that distinct regional variations existed in the regional incidence of unfit housing in 1971. As Table 7.3 reveals, the proportion of unfit dwellings was considerably below average in the South-east of England and most severe in the old industrial areas of the North of England – those areas comprising the Northern, Yorkshire and Humberside and the

Table 7.3 Unfit dwellings in England and Wales in 1971 by region, age and tenure

ENGLAND AND WALES	PROPORTION OF UNFIT DWELLINGS 7.3	PROPORTION OF NOT UNFIT DWELLINGS 92.7
Region		
Northern, Yorkshire and Humberside and North-west	10.1	89.9
South-east	4.0	96.0
Rest of England and Wales	8.0	92.0
Age		
Pre-1919	21.6	78.4
1919 to 1971	0.4	99.6
Tenure		
Owner-occupied	3.9	96.1
Rented from local authorities or new towns	1.2	98.8
other tenures	22.9	77.1
Closed	100.0	—
Vacant	39.5	60.5

Source: Department of the Environment (1973a, pp. 12 and 13).

North West economic planning regions. Most of the dwellings classified, in 1971, as being unfit were built prior to 1919 and slightly more than one-fifth of all pre-1919 properties were found to be unfit for continued occupation. Only about 15 per cent of these unfit dwellings were vacant or had been closed under the various housing and town planning acts, however; the remainder were still being occupied at the time of the survey. Not surprisingly, perhaps, the incidence of unfit property was higher in the private, rather than in the public sector, though it is noticeable that some 58 000 local authority and new town properties (1.2 per cent of the total dwelling stock) were officially regarded as being unsuitable for continued occupation. Most of these (86 per cent) were constructed prior to 1919. In the private sector, unfit dwellings constituted slightly less than 4 per cent of the owner-occupier market and nearly all of these (97 per cent) were built in the pre-1919 period. By far the highest proportion of occupied unfit dwellings was in the 'other' tenure category and many of these would be properties rented from a private landlord – the type of dwelling traditionally regarded as the basis of the slum.

On the basis of the statistics available, therefore, it would appear that, far from being of uniform proportions, the problem of unfit housing is extremely varied and the country is faced not with a singular problem of unfit housing but with a series of problems which vary in severity from area to area.

CHAPTER 8
THE POLICIES OF SUCCESSIVE
BRITISH GOVERNMENTS

Chapters 4, 5 and 6 outlined the three major policies (filtering, redevelopment and rehabilitation) for raising the standard of housing conditions and eliminating slum property. In an analysis of British housing policy, it is possible to identify the operation of all three. At different periods in time, the emphasis has changed from one to another as a result of Government legislation and, in the past fifty years or so, the financial subsidies which the central Government has given to both local authorities and private bodies. In the context of these policies, it is possible to identify two major watersheds in the British attempt to alleviate the problem of slum housing in England and Wales. Prior to 1930, the main drive was to improve the general housing situation and the Government relied largely upon the filtering process to eliminate slum housing and improve the quality of the housing stock. From 1930 to 1965, the Government pinned its faith on slum clearance, while from 1965 onwards, increased emphasis has been placed on residential rehabilitation. While these dates permit the identification of periods in British social history when each of the policies was dominant, it must be appreciated that the periods are not exclusive; filtering did not end in 1930 and rehabilitation did not begin in 1965. Throughout the three periods, each of the policies has occurred to a greater or lesser extent. What is more, it must be appreciated that since a dwelling can be regarded as being unfit as a consequence of both the standard of accommodation provided by the dwelling itself and the quality of the residential environment, legislation has taken two forms: the first has related to individual unfit dwellings while the second has related to areas of slum conditions. Once again, the legislation has tended to emphasise each of these approaches at different times. To facilitate analysis, however, attention has been focused on the primary policy divisions relating to the methods of eliminating slum housing and raising the standard of accommodation.

PRE-1930, THE ERA OF RESIDENTIAL FILTERING

While the origins of the modern clearance and rehabilitation programmes have their roots in the legislation of the late nineteenth and early twentieth centuries, neither policy had any major impact on the problem of slum housing during this period. In 1868, the Artisans' and Labourers' Dwelling Act (the Torrens Act) was passed and local authorities were empowered to require the owners of property to undertake repairs to their premises. If this was not done, the authorities could close any dwelling which they felt was so dangerous to health as to be unfit for human habitation and to require that the owner have it demolished at his or her expense. Under the Torrens Act, neither rehousing nor demolition was the responsibility of the local authority.

While the Torrens Act dealt with individual unfit housing, the Artisans' and Labourers' Dwellings Improvement Act, 1875, related to areas of unfit housing. Basically the act was concerned with the clearance of an area and its ultimate redevelopment. Under Section 3, an authority could declare an improvement area (currently termed a clearance area) in those instances where 'houses, courts, or alleys . . . are unfit for human habitation, or . . . diseases indicating a generally low condition of health amongst the population have been from time to time prevalent . . . and . . . such prevalence may be reasonably attributed to the closeness, narrowness, and bad arrangement or the bad condition of the streets and houses . . . or to the want of light, air, ventilation, or proper conveniences or to any other sanitary defects . . .'. In 1890, these conditions were modified, under Section 4(b) of the Housing of the Working Classes Act, so that an unhealthy area was defined as any area 'dangerous or injurious to the health of the inhabitants'.

Under the 1875 Act, the Local Government Board could issue a provisional order designating the area for improvement but this had to be confirmed by an act of Parliament before work could commence. Not until the Housing, Town Planning, etc. Act of 1909 was the need for Parliamentary approval withdrawn. Unlike the Torrens Act of 1868, Section 5 of the 1875 Act required that an improvement scheme should '. . . provide for the accommodation of at least as many members of the working class as may be displaced . . . in suitable dwellings, which, unless there are any special reasons to the contrary, shall be situated within the limits of the same area, or in the vicinity thereof . . .'. Because of the costs of land and building, however, these rehousing requirements proved to be a major disincentive to local authorities and the Act was modified in 1879 to allow replacement housing to be provided at some location other than the area cleared or the immediate vicinity. Moreover, a further amendment in 1882 made rehousing discretionary outside London.

Perhaps the next major development in British housing policy came in 1919 with the Housing, Town Planning, etc. Act. This took the somewhat revolutionary step of providing an Exchequer subsidy for local authority housebuilding. Although the subsidy was intended to stimulate housebuilding to provide 'Homes Fit for Heroes' in a period of rapid inflation, it was available for slum clearance programmes. However, the Government felt that 'it would obviously be unwise to attempt to put into operation drastic measures for clearing unhealthy areas' (Ministry of Health, 1921, p. 71) until the shortage of housing accommodation, resulting from the First World War, had been remedied. Not only did the Act provide subsidies for general housebuilding and slum clearance purposes, but it also empowered local authorities to acquire, alter, enlarge, repair and improve accommodation and to lend money to private owners for improvement or conversion works. Indeed, the Ministry of Health Circular (17/19) of 29 July 1919, urged local authorities to prepare schemes and to survey their districts for property suitable for conversion. Further stimulus to improvement was given under the Housing (Rural Workers) Act of 1928. This empowered local authorities outside London to make improvement grants for improvement work costing £50 or more. A grant of two-thirds the cost of the work could be given up to a £100 maximum but, in order that the benefits of the act should be restricted to the working classes, the value of the improved cottage was not to exceed £400 and the tenancy was to be reserved for an agricultural, or similar status, worker for a period of twenty years.

While the 1926 Act attempted to stimulate improvement, the Housing Act of 1923 reduced the subsidy on slum clearance and although the various acts of the period 1919–30 contained provisions for the clearance of slums and the improvement of accommodation, it is generally agreed that the programmes of the period were intended to reduce the housing shortage and to raise the general standard of accommodation for the working classes. Prior to 1930, as the Ministry of Health (1931, p. 98) recognised, 'the policy previously followed by all Governments had been to concentrate almost exclusively on the provision of new houses in order to increase the total pool of accommodation available for the working classes; and, while a limited amount of slum clearance was undertaken under the Housing Acts from 1890 to 1925, it was considered that any direct and comprehensive plan to clear the slums and to meet the needs of the poorest workers must meanwhile be deferred. It was, however, hoped and expected that their conditions would be indirectly improved by a general process which has been described as "filtering up".'

1930–1969, THE ERA OF SLUM CLEARANCE

It has already been emphasised that the 1930 Housing Act (the Greenwood Act) was the foundation of Britain's modern slum clearance programmes. Basically the Act attempted, as the Minister for Health outlined during the second reading of the bill, to reduce the procedural complexities involved in slum clearance and to make clearance more attractive, financially. Under the Act, the procedures for clearing an area were separated from those involved in redeveloping the site. Provisions were introduced for the clearance of individual unfit houses but of even greater significance, perhaps, was the introduction of a system of compulsory purchase and clearance orders. This system has remained virtually unchanged over the past forty years or more. Financially, the subsidies paid under the Greenwood Act were considerably more favourable than had been the subsidies for slum clearance under previous housing acts. Whereas previous financial assistance was based on the loss incurred by a local authority, the new subsidies were calculated on the number of persons displaced. For every person rehoused, the basic subsidy was £2 5s. 0d. (£2.25) for forty years.

While the 1930 Housing Act was intended to give impetus to the slum clearance programme, it was not intended that subsidised building for general needs should cease. However, in 1933, the general needs subsidy was abolished by the Housing (Financial Provisions) Act of that year and the Government embarked upon a drive to rid the country of its slum properties by 1938. On 6 April 1933, this policy was brought to the attention of the housing authorities in England and Wales through the publication of the Ministry of Health Circular 1331. 'In this, the authorities were informed that, in the view of the Government, the rate at which slums were being dealt with was too slow; and that a concerted effort between the Central Government and the local authorities was necessary to ensure a speedier end to the evil. . . .' (Ministry of Health, 1934, p. 2.)

The Government's new housing policy was summarised in the report of the Departmental Committee on Housing. This stated that the intention was 'to concentrate public effort and money on the clearance and improvement of slum conditions, and to rely in the main on competitive private enterprise to provide a new supply of accommodation for the working classes . . .' (Ministry of Health, 1933, p. 4). Clearly, the Government recognised that the elimination of slum housing could not be left to the filtering process but it would also appear that it expected the provision of new housing to raise the general standard of working-class accommodation. The filtering process would complement the slum clearance drive.

The introduction, in 1935, of a scheme to abolish the related problem of over-crowding gave further impetus to the slum clearance campaign. Under Section 1 of the Housing Act, 1935, local authorities were instructed to survey the extent of overcrowding in their areas and to prepare plans for the provision of accommodation. Clearly, many of the families living in overcrowded conditions would also be living in slum properties, so the relief of overcrowding might, for some households, mean a movement from the slums. Of more importance from the slum clearance aspect was the fact that subsidies for the abatement of overcrowding were lower than those for slum clearance. Consequently, if an overcrowded family could be dealt with under the slum clearance programme, the local authority received a larger subsidy from the Treasury than if it were dealt with under the decrowding programme. As Bowley (1945, p. 152) observes 'there is not the slightest doubt that where there was a possibility of choice as to the subsidy under which families could be rehoused, they were included in the slum clearance schemes'. This distinction was removed on 1 January 1939, when the two subsidies were assimilated under the Housing (Finance Provisions) Act, 1938.

With the advent of the Second World War, the slum clearance campaign came to an abrupt halt and was not resumed until 1954. During the war, building and maintenance virtually ceased with the result that, by 1945, the slum problem was undoubtedly worse than it had been in 1939. The shortage of housing was so acute, however, that 'even a slum house was better than being homeless' (English and Norman, 1974, p. 14). As a consequence, the slum clearance programme was suspended, but the Government, recognising the need to prevent further deterioration of the dwelling stock, introduced the system of improvement grants which forms the foundation of the present-day improvement programme. Under the Housing Act of 1949, grants of up to 50 per cent of the cost of improvement were made available for work costing between £100 and £600, providing that the dwellings had an anticipated life of at least thirty years and for twenty years the rent increase was limited to 6 per cent of the landlord's contribution. Where the property was owner-occupied, resale limitations were imposed. In 1952, the cost limitations were increased to work costing between £150 and £800 under the Housing (Improvements Grants) (Expenses) Regulations but the property was expected to provide accommodation for at least fifty years.

In the debate on the Queen's Speech in November 1953, the Minister for Housing and Local Government, Mr Harold Macmillan, pointed out that although the country was still faced with 'the great problem of overcrowding, of families with no home of their own . . . we can no longer afford to put off, to put aside, the question of the slums. We can no longer leave people living in cramped, dark, rotten houses with no water, sometimes no lavatories, no proper ventilation and no hope of rescue' (House of Commons, 1953, col. 188). In his, and the Government's view 'the time had come to take it [the slum problem] up again as a great National effort' (House of Commons, 1953, col. 187). The Government's programme was outlined in the White Paper *Houses – the Next Step*, released during the debate. This introduced the Government's Better Housing Campaign and pointed out that although the need for slum clearance was urgent, it was 'not the intention that the whole of the local authority's effort should be switched to the demolition and replacement of slums' (Ministry of Housing and Local Government, 1953, p. 11). The housing stock was divided into four categories – slum, dilapidated, improvable and essentially sound – and different policies were planned for each group. It has already been observed that, as in the 1930s, local authorities were required to submit programmes for the clearance of the slum properties within their areas. Where it was impossible to eliminate all slum properties within five years, new powers of deferred demolition were to be available for the acquisition and 'patching' of dwellings. Local authorities were to be authorised to enforce substantial repairs to dilapidated property and if a landlord failed to ensure that the dwelling was 'fit for human habitation', the work could be done by the local authority or the property could be demolished. In an attempt to prolong the useful life of many improvable dwellings, it was planned that the £800 ceiling on the cost of improvement work should be removed, though the maximum grant should remain at 50 per cent of the cost of the approved expenditure. Finally, since the maintenance of much privately rented accommodation had been neglected since the Second World War, the Government planned to increase the rents of essentially sound housing to encourage landlords to make repairs.

Naturally, such proposals, particularly the latter, brought considerable protest from the Opposition. The statutory powers needed to implement the White Paper were provided by the Housing Repairs and Rents Act 1954, and apart from the deferred demolition procedure, the Act made only minor changes to the slum clearance law. As outlined in Chapter 7, a new fitness standard was introduced under Section 9 of the Act, the £800 ceiling on improvements was removed and the 6 per cent maximum rent increase allowed by the 1949 Act was raised to 8 per cent. The Government believed that the solution to the problem of slum housing lay predominantly in slum clearance. Accordingly, it pledged itself 'to secure, as soon as possible the rehousing of at least 200 000 people a year, involving the annual provision of about 60 000 new dwellings for this purpose' (House of Commons, 1955, cols. 176–7). At the same time, however, it is apparent that the Government also recognised that if the slum clearance campaign was to have an impact on the slum problem, it had to be complemented by a vigorous programme of maintenance, repair and improvement. While the slum clearance drive of the mid-1950s 'followed closely the lines of the 1930s campaign' (English and Norman, 1974, p. 19), it differed from the earlier programme in its reliance on rehabilitation, rather than filtering, as a complementary method of combating the problem.

Once the clearance programme had become established in 1954, only minor policy modifications took place until 1956 when, under the Housing Subsidies Act of that year, a further boost was given to the slum clearance campaign by the abolition of the general needs subsidy. Eventually, the various measures responsible for effecting slum clearance were consolidated under the Housing Act 1957. In the following year, the Housing (Financial Provisions) Act 1958, as amended by the House Purchase and Housing Act of 1959, introduced the system of discretionary improvement grants. By 1959, therefore, both standard and discretionary grants were being paid in an attempt to stimulate the rehabilitation of residential accommodation.

Perhaps the first major jolt to the clearance policy of the 1950s came in 1960 with the publication of Cullingworth's book *Housing Needs and Planning Policy*. In this, Cullingworth (1960) pointed out that the 1954 local authority returns were a gross underestimate of the extent of the slum problem, demonstrated the on-going nature of the problem and argued that more emphasis ought to be placed on a policy of subsidised rehabilitation. Cullingworth's conclusions were supported in the following year by Needleman (1961) in his paper 'A long term view of housing' and by the findings of Burnett and Scott (1962) in their 1960 survey of housing conditions in the urban areas of England and Wales. With the publication, in May 1962, of the Government commissioned Social Survey report on the housing situation in 1960 (Gray and Russell, 1962), the Government had official confirmation of the failure of its slum clearance programme. It responded by initiating a special drive in those areas where the problem was known to be most acute and by placing greater emphasis on improvement. In the *Improvement of Houses* (Circular 42/62, published on 2 August 1962) the Ministry of Housing and Local Government advised local authorities that the Government was anxious to promote large-scale house improvements and was willing to sanction loans and compulsory purchase orders for the purchase of property which required improvement. These points were repeated in the White Paper *Housing* (Cmnd 2050) published during the following year. The provisions outlined in the paper were subsequently embodied in the Housing Act, 1964. Under the Act, no new sources of finance were provided but tenanted dwellings could be compulsorily improved to the level of the standard grant on both an area and piecemeal basis.

By the end of 1964, therefore, it is possible to see the beginnings of a move away from slum clearance towards the rehabilitation or improvement of both dwellings and areas. While the 1964 Act did not include any special measures for environmental improvement, circular 53/64 made it clear that the improvement of environmental conditions sould not be neglected.

1965 TO THE PRESENT: THE ERA OF REHABILITATION

In the White Paper, *The Housing Programme, 1965 to 1970*, the Government stated that its first objective was to produce half a million houses a year by 1970, though it recognised that even this would be inadequate, 'partly because of the accumulated pressure of bad and insufficient housing, partly because as standards of living rise, families will demand and be prepared to pay for more space and better housing' (Ministry of Housing and Local Government, 1965, p. 3). While the Paper was concerned, primarily, with the housebuilding programme, it stressed the importance of more effort being devoted to improving the conditions of existing houses and pointed out that the Government would 'encourage local authorities to greater efforts in promoting house improvement coupled with improvement of whole areas – including better street lighting, play areas, parking space and so on' (Ministry of Housing and Local Government, 1965, pp. 15 and 16). The Government was not thinking simply of the improvement of areas of property but of improving both the property and the residential environment.

One of the major conclusions of the White Paper was that 'for a comprehensive and firmly based plan much more must be known about the reality of housing needs . . .' (Ministry of Housing and Local Government, 1965, p. 16) and that far too little research had been done. In accordance with this belief, the Dennington Committee had been appointed in February 1965 to consider, as mentioned previously, 'the practicability of specifying objective criteria for the purposes of slum clearance, rectification of disrepair and other housing powers relating to minimum tolerable standards of housing accommodation' (Central Housing Advisory Committee, 1966, p. 1). Among its twenty conclusions, the Committee recommended that there was a need for more research into the criteria for achieving the most economic allocation of resources between replacement and improvement, for effective compulsion to improve and maintain the better old houses, for local authorities to have a duty to clear houses where living conditions were made intolerable by bad environmental conditions, for local authorities to be given the necessary powers to secure the proper maintenance of all dwellings, for the necessary resources to be channelled to those authorities with the most serious slum problems, for the extension of the existing arrangements for mandatory improvement grants and loans and, finally, for more information. Over the succeeding years, these recommendations were to have an important influence on Government policy. Almost immediately, the last recommendation was met, in part, by the 1967 House Condition Survey (Ministry of Housing and Local Government, 1968b) while the 1967 Housing Act gave more generous subsidies to 'priority' areas and provided increased subsidies for the purchase, improvement or conversion of property by private housing associations. In October 1967, however, Circular 69/67 announced that the Government intended to review its housing legislation and in April 1968, this review appeared, together with the results of the 1967 House Condition Survey, as the White Paper *Old Houses into New Homes* (Ministry of Housing and Local Government, 1968a). As the title implies, the Paper announced that, in future, a greater share of the total public investment in housing would go to the improvement of older homes and outlined the Government's policy for area and house improvement as well as slum clearance. The Paper indicated that the area improvement provisions of the 1964 Act were to be replaced by a system for the declaration of General Improvement Areas (GIA), while the powers to compel owners to repair their property were to be extended. In addition, the maximum level of the discretionary grant was to be raised from £400 to £1 000 and the ceiling for standard grants from £150 to £200, while it was intended to increase the maximum grant from £500 to £1 200. As the White Paper recognised, these increases reflected 'not only increases in prices . . . but the Government's view of what it may in certain cases be worthwhile to spend on improving or converting a house' (Ministry of Housing and Local Government, 1968a, p. 5). Further aid was to be given in the form of assistance towards the purchase of property for improvement or conversion. This would be paid to local authorities and housing associations alike and the ceiling was to be raised from £2 000 to £2 500.

The statutory powers for these proposals were provided by the Housing Act, 1969. When the Act was passed in July of that year, it marked a new era in British housing policy: the drive to rehabilitate and improve both residential properties and the environments in which these properties were situated. As the 1968 White Paper outlined, 'the Government want local authorities to direct their main efforts in future to the improvement of whole areas, not just individual houses.' (Ministry of Housing and Local Government, 1968a, p. 3.) Although this was the intention, there were no financial incentives for local authorities to designate improvement areas – grants were available in General Improvement areas on the same basis as elsewhere. It was not until the Housing Act of 1971 that variable improvement grants were introduced. Under the Act, grants of 75 per cent of the 'approved' expenditure on improvement could be paid in intermediate and development areas and in such cases the Exchequer contribution was to be 90 per cent of the grant. In other areas, the maximum was no more than 50 per cent of the approved expenditure with a 75 per cent Exchequer contribution. Everywhere in the country, the maximum grant remained at £1 000 or £1 200 for three-storey or converted property. Clearly the Act recognised the variable character of the housing problem in England and Wales and was attempting to provide maximum assistance for those authorities most in need. As the Rt Hon Julian Amery observed in 1972 'we are faced not so much by a national housing problem as by a series of local housing problems, many radically different and each varying in its nature and the range of possible solutions.' (Department of the Environment, 1972, Annexe B.) The measures were not sufficiently flexible, however, and, as Roberts (1976, p. 32) has pointed out in his recent review of the General Improvement Area concept, they were 'applied to regions defined in terms of economic rather than housing deficiencies; indeed, it was partly an attempt to increase employment'. In June 1974, the measures were discontinued but it did not mean that the Government had abandoned its policy of providing assistance to those areas most in need. In the 1973 White Paper *Better Homes: the Next Priorities,* the Government stressed that it was necessary 'to redirect the priorities and emphases of improvement policy to ensure that help is directed more purposefully to those areas where the worst housing problems are increasingly concentrated' (Department of the Environment, 1973b, p. 4).

Throughout the early 1970s, criticism of the General Improvement Area programme had been increasing. Roberts (1976, pp. 33 and 34) summarises these critic-isms as follows: 'GIAs suffer from three main criticisms:

1. an attempt to impose a relatively uniform, relatively high standard of improvement on areas with possibly mixed social requirements, which thus makes GIAs potentially antisocial;
2. too limited in scale to tackle a national housing problem;
3. too broad in scale and conception to tackle areas of housing stress.'

Despite these criticisms, the 1973 White Paper recommended the retention of the General Improvement Area programme and proposed a rate of improvement grant higher than that generally available 'so as to make more impact on the quality of the environment of older residential districts in those many parts of England and Wales free from housing stress' (Department of the Environment, 1973b, p. 9). The main feature of the White Paper was the proposal for the creation of Housing Action Areas (HAA) – areas in which it would be possible for local authorities to give special repair-only and preferential improvement grants. Within these areas, local authorities could apply all of their existing powers and, in addition, would be able to:

(a) compel minimum standards of improvement and repair;
(b) attach conditions to the payment of improvement grants to ensure that improved rented accommodation was kept available for letting at registered rates;
(c) require the vendors of rented accommodation to give first refusal to either an approved housing association or the authority itself;
(d) nominate a tenant for vacant rented accommodation where it was clear that the landlord was not trying to fill the vacancy;
(e) award grants above the preferential rate in cases of undue hardship.

In creating the Housing Action Area, the Government was attempting 'to give priority to the task of dealing comprehensively with the physical conditions in the remaining areas of worst housing and to help those people suffering hardship arising from these conditions' (Department of the Environment, 1973b, p. 5). Accordingly the Paper proposed that the criteria for defining these areas should be related to both social and housing factors; it included overcrowded conditions, shared accommodation, concent-rations of elderly people and large families, furnished tenancies and dwellings lacking such basic amenities as a hot water supply, fixed bath or inside toilet.

Although the intention was to introduce 'early legislation', it was some eighteen months before the proposals reached the statute books. Under the provisions of the Housing Act, 1974, improvement grants of up to 50 per cent of the cost of approved expenditure could be paid and the Exchequer contribution would be 75 per cent of the grant. In General Improvement Areas, grants of up to 60 per cent of the cost of improvement were payable with 90 per cent of the funding coming from the Exchequer. In Housing Action Areas, grants of between 75 and 90 per cent of the expenditure on improvement could be paid and the Exchequer contribution was 90 per cent of the grant.

CONCLUSION

Over the past one hundred years or so, the policies of successive British Governments towards the problem of slum properties have revealed a shift in emphasis from reliance upon the filtering process through a programme of almost total dependence on slum clearance to a programme of rehabilitation backed by slum clearance. To some, these changes in policy might be seen as a reflection of the changing nature of the problem; either, a perceived reduction in the scale of the problem enables less emphasis to be placed on slum clearance programmes or, as was the case during the immediate post-Second World War period, the general shortage of accommodation makes it difficult to justify the removal of any property from the dwelling stock. While these factors have had an undoubted effect on British housing policy, other factors have been of significant importance. In the late 1920s it became apparent that the problem of slum housing could not be resolved without direct Government intervention and in 1930 the first slum clearance drive was initiated. This was in keeping with the notion that housing policy should be geared principally to public health considerations and to the improvement of working-class living conditions and life-styles. In recent years programmes of wide-spread demolition and replacement have become less and less popular as many of the problems outlined earlier have become more fully appreciated. Indeed, it has been argued that 'many of our present difficulties undoubtedly stem from the mistake we made in the 1950s and 1960s of believing we could bulldoze our housing problems out of the way by demolition and new building alone.' (Crosland, 1976, p. 118.) It has been increasingly realised that the problem of slum property is on-going and it is not only necessary to rid the country of its worst housing but, at the same time, to retard the rate at which dwellings become obsolete. Accordingly, the 1969 Housing Act initiated a major programme of modernisation and improvement. It soon became obvious, however, that the improvement grant system was insufficiently discriminating; not only were grants frequently being used to improve second homes or to benefit speculators, but it was apparent that the housing problem was not uniform throughout the country and resources were not being directed to those places and to those people most in need. At the same time, there has been a reaction to the largely physical bias in British housing policy and it became equally clear that insufficient consideration had been given to the effects of the 1969 Act improvement grant provisions on the tenants of improved property. The Housing Act, 1974, was therefore, 'an attempt to redress the balance to bring human considerations more positively into the reckoning and to deal more effectively with housing stress' (Freeson, 1975, p.2012).

CHAPTER 9
THE ACHIEVEMENTS
OF SUCCESSIVE
BRITISH GOVERNMENTS

As Mansell (1972, p. 77) has observed 'one of the few things over which housing experts are in perfect accord is that this country (Britain) has a housing problem not very close to solution.' Given the policies of successive British Governments over the past one hundred years or more, presumably the situation can be explained, at least in part, by the title of Mansell's paper – 'The perpetual housing problem'. Previous chapters have stressed this point. The problem of slum housing is on-going. As living standards have risen and the worst housing conditions have been removed, so there has occurred a corresponding rise in the standard which society has deemed to be acceptable for human habitation. Undoubtedly there are other reasons. In his book, *Housing: the Great British Failure,* Berry (1974) goes one step further. He argues that, far from improving, the British housing problem is getting worse and suggests that part of the blame for this failure must rest with the policies of the central Government which have 'flitted from one palliative to another' (Berry, 1974, p. 224). What Berry is suggesting is that national housing policies have suffered from lack of continuity and have tended to alleviate the symptoms rather than cure the cause. The evidence provided in Chapter 8 does not appear to support the former contention. The implementation of three policies over the last one hundred years or so would seem to suggest a fairly stable approach but lack of continuity is certainly one of the features of the British political system. Between October 1900 and October 1974, there were some twenty-one general elections and the average life of a British Parliament was approximately three and a half years. What is more, twelve of these twenty-one elections resulted in a change of Government. Given the ideological differences of the two major British political parties and the disruptive effect of elections on the governance of a country, it is only to be expected that housing policy, like other central government policies, would be affected.

The question of the inappropriateness of Government policy has already been alluded to. In Chapter 8, for instance, reference was made to Crosland's views of the effects of slum clearance. Equally, the rehabilitation programme has been severely criticised. For instance, it is argued that the improvement of older housing is no more than a relatively short-term palliative; that the great majority of improved property will require replacement between 1980 and 1995. This argument is taken up by Berry (1974, pp. 205-6) who argues that 'the commitment to a rehabilitation policy is a vast exercise in putting off the evil day and not putting it off for very long.'

Opinions about the effectiveness of British housing policy are highly divided. The aim of this chapter is, therefore, to examine the effectiveness of the legislation and, where appropriate, to demonstrate its inherent weaknesses.

PRE-1930

Compared with more recent legislation for dealing with slum property, the pre-1930 legislation was largely ineffective. There were several reasons for this, but the main factors are outlined by English and Norman. In their view 'there is little doubt that the principal reason for the poor performance was the high cost of improvement schemes. After some initial enthusiasm local authorities soon realised the implications of improvements for the rates; there were a number of instances of local authorities refusing to act on official representations by medical officers of health. Parliament attempted to reduce costs mainly by abandoning the rehousing requirement rather than curbing compensation. The few voices calling for State subsidies were not taken seriously before 1914. The tentative steps towards simplifying improvement procedures were no more effective and those schemes which were started often dragged on interminably.' (English and Norman, 1974, p. 6.) The ineffectiveness of the pre-1930 legislation appears to have stemmed from the cost of improvement to the local authoritiy, the rehousing obligation and the complexity of the improvement procedure. Moreover, as Bowley (1945, p. 3) has observed, official housing policy in the period prior to the First World War 'was limited to making it legally possible for the local sanitary authorities to deal with the slums at their own expense, if they liked'. The legislation did not compel local authorities to eradicate slum housing or to provide improved accommodation. What is more, the legislation was largely negative, concerned with preventing or destroying insanitary conditions rather than creating good housing. Rarely did the legislation bring about any real improvement in the housing of the working classes. For instance, 'the Improvement Acts of Torrens and Cross, although they were pioneering attempts at lifting the conditions of the people, in fact increased the misery of the cities. By allowing and encouraging the demolition of homes without a rehousing policy they inevitably increased overcrowding and the ills attendant upon it.' (Gauldie, 1974, p. 267.)

After the First World War, housing policy became more positive as the Government attempted to stimulate housebuilding and to provide 'Homes fit for Heroes'. The main purpose of the legislation was to encourage the building of additional houses. Although the powers of local authorities to clear slums and force landlords to repair and improve their property were marginally strengthened, authorities were under no obligation and there was little pressure from either the public or the Ministry of Health; concern was focused predominantly on the absolute shortage of accommodation. Even so, there was a gradual increase in the volume of slum clearance up to 1928 'Each year between two thousand and five thousand houses were subject to closing and demolition orders. As far as unhealthy areas were concerned, between 1919 and 1928 121 improvement schemes were confirmed involving the demolition of about 15 000 buildings and the rehousing of approximately 74 000 persons. But only about 11 000 houses included in these had actually been demolished by 1930.' (English, Madigan and Norman, 1976, p. 19.)

Progress was brought to an abrupt halt in 1928, however, by an application to the King's Bench Division for a wait of prohibition. The application was allowed and confirmed by the Court of Appeal. As is made clear in the Ministry of Health report for 1929–30, the judgement made it impossible for the Minister of Health 'to approve any of the schemes before him, or any of the eleven which local authorities have since submitted' (Ministry of Health, 1930, p. 83). By 1930, therefore, 'only 17 000 persons had been rehoused under slum clearance schemes' (Bowley, 1945, p. 147) and about 300 000 dwellings had been made fit by reconditioning.

Not only did the judgement halt progress in dealing with slum properties, but it brought about a fundamental reappraisal of the legislative framework relating to slum clearance. For some time, the Government had recognised 'that fresh procedures and fresh methods [were] required to enable local authorities to remedy slums' (Ministry of Health, 1930, p. 83). The result was the slum clearance legislation of 1930.

1930–1965

While the 1930 Act removed many of the obstacles to slum clearance experienced previously, there is little doubt that, up to 1933, it was a failure. As was pointed out in Chapter 7, the programmes put forward by the main local authorities in England and Wales in response to the 1930 Act proposed the demolition of only 76 524 dwellings. At contemporary building rates, this number of properties could have been provided within eighteen months. By December 1933, only 11 796 dwellings had actually been constructed and it is perfectly clear that the local authorities were not cooperating with the central Government in its drive to rid the country of its slum properties. Bowley explains this in terms of the inadequacy of the subsidy and the fact that a general building subsidy was also available. Given the somewhat conservative nature of the original estimates, it might be argued that the local authorities did not share the Government's enthusiasm for the slum clearance programme; some local authorities might not have appreciated the magnitude of the problem, some might have opposed the policy or been politically opposed to the Government and all of its policies, while others might have been influenced by local dignitaries with a vested interest in slum property. Whatever the reason, it is as clear now as it was in 1933, that the rate of progress was too slow.

Reference has been made earlier to the inauguration, in 1933, of the major slum clearance drive and to the measures taken by the central Government to stimulate progress. Although the local authority returns were an underestimate of the magnitude of the problem, the campaign to eradicate all slum properties was clearly less than successful (Table 9.1). By 1939, not all of the dwellings included in the 1934 programme had been demolished and it would appear that not only did the Government fail to ensure that the local authorities prepared accurate estimates, but it also failed to stimulate many authorities to carry out their programmes. At the outset, the Ministry of Health never believed that the 'big five' (London, Birmingham, Leeds, Liverpool and Manchester) could complete their programmes within five years and by the end of 1939, 'the unfulfilled programmes of the "big five" accounted for the greater part of the gap between original programmes and completed programmes. But the "big five" were not alone in their failure; at least ten other county boroughs failed to complete their programmes as well as some of the smaller towns and industrialised urban and rural areas.' (Bowley, 1945, p. 155.) Indeed, 'recalcitrant authorities remained able to abstain from slum clearance.' (op. cit., 1945, p. 159.) Even so, more slum families were rehoused in the five-year period, 1934–39, than had been rehoused under all of the official clearance schemes since 1890 and some 751 000 dwellings had been rendered fit for human habitation since 1930.

Immediately prior to the Second World War approximately 90 000 dwellings were being demolished each year. During the six years which the war lasted, little more than 68 000 properties were closed or demolished and even repairs were rarely undertaken. After 1945, clearance was not resumed until 1954 and only 96 808 demolitions or closures were undertaken during this ten-year period. In effect, the Second World War brought about not only 'a postponement of slum clearance, but also an enforced neglect of existing houses for over fourteen years' (Cullingworth, 1966, p. 191). As was pointed

Table 9.1   Slum clearance programmes of local authorities, England and Wales, 1930–1939

Number of dwellings to be closed or demolished:	
January 1934	266 851
March 1939	472 000
Number of dwellings actually closed or demolished:	
1930 to March 1934	27 564
April 1934 to March 1939	245 272
Total, 1930 to 1939	272 836
Deficit in progress, 1934 to 1939:	
(a) 1934 programme	21 579
(b) 1939 programme	266 728

Source: Bowley (1945, p. 153)

out in the previous chapter, the second slum clearance drive, which closely followed the lines of the 1930s campaign, was initiated in 1954. In circular 55/54 (published 28 August 1954), the Ministry of Housing and Local Government instructed that, within twelve months, all of the local authorities in England and Wales should submit programmes for ministerial approval. It has already been demonstrated that, as was the case some twenty years previously, many local authorities underestimated the magnitude of the problem. Unlike the situation experienced earlier, many responded to the Government's attempts to stimulate clearance and did not wait for ministerial approval before commencing. Indeed, 'from 1 January to 30 November 1954, local authorities in England and Wales submitted 298 slum clearance compulsory purchase orders and 228 clearance orders.' (House of Commons, 1954, col. 1 567.)

It has been pointed out that in 1954 it was conservatively estimated that there were some 847 112 dwellings in England and Wales which were unfit for habitation and some 375 484 of these required demolition within five years. It has also been pointed out that the aim of the Government was to rehouse at least 200 000 people each year and to provide 60 000 new dwellings per year for slum clearance purposes. With a renewal rate of 60 000 dwellings a year, it would take more than six years to replace those dwellings requiring immediate demolition and at least fourteen years to rid the country of all of the slum properties identified in 1954. In reality, the Government never achieved its objective of rehousing 200 000 people a year (Table 9.2) and in April 1958, it was calculated that, at the prevailing rate of progress, it would take twenty-nine years to clear the 847 112 unfit dwellings identified in 1954 (House of Commons, 1958, cols. 1 010 and 1 011). While there appears to have been some error in the calculation, it is obvious that the local authorities were not achieving the progress which the Government expected. What is more, even the projected rate of action was too slow and in 1960, it was calculated that 'a desirable rate of demolition would probably be of the order of 200 000 houses a year.' (Cullingworth, 1960, p. 53.) With demolition rates running at around 60 000 dwellings per annum, such a rate was clearly unattainable, as was the rate of 130 000 units per annum suggested in 1962 by Gray and Russell; the local authorities simply did not possess the financial, technical and physical resources to deal with redevelopment at the pace required and the national legislation failed to provide adequate incentives for those authorities in whose areas the problem was most

Table 9.2   Slum clearance in England and Wales, 1954–1964

YEAR	DWELLINGS CLOSED OR DEMOLISHED	PERSONS MOVED
1955	26 023	79 965
1956	36 336	115 093
1957	47 015	159 223
1958	55 273	159 923
1959	60 205	156 642
1960	56 561	165 607
1961	61 969	165 838
1962	61 842	168 809
1963	61 428	162 066
1964	61 215	159 890

Source: Cullingworth (1966, p. 190)

severe. Given the evidence, the conclusion of Mr Michael Steward (MP for Fulham) seems inescapable; the country was 'not clearing slums as fast as the passage of time (was) creating new ones' (House of Commons, 1964, cols. 1 402 and 1 403).

1965 TO THE PRESENT

The point has been made that, in an attempt to retard the rate at which slum properties are formed, emphasis since 1964 has been placed on rehabilitation. As can be seen from Table 9.3 very few dwellings were improved or converted during the decade 1949–59 and throughout the early 1960s only about 120 000 dwellings were improved each year. Despite the Government's intention to 'encourage local authorities to greater efforts in promoting house improvement' (Ministry of Housing and Local Government, 1965, p. 15), the late 1960s actually witnessed a decline in the number of grant-aided

Table 9.3 Grant-aided improvements and conversions, England and Wales, 1949–1964

	IMPROVEMENTS			CONVERSIONS	TOTAL
	Standard	Discretionary	Total		
1949–59	33,061	220 656	220 656	18 209	238 865
1960	82 819	42 988	125 807	5 025	130 832
1961	79,831	42 808	122 639	5 137	127 776
1962	68 738	36 835	105 573	4 933	110 506
1963	77 278	37 563	114 841	5 133	119 974
1964	76 635	40 072	116 707	4 978	121 685

Source: Cullingworth (1966, p. 216)

Table 9.4 Grant-aided improvements and conversions, England and Wales, 1965–1975

	STANDARD	DISCRETIONARY	TOTAL
1965	82 893	40 100	122 993
1966	67 760	39 960	107 720
1967	66 536	46 606	113 142
1968	68 038	46 178	114 216
1969	59 562	49 376	108 938
1970	69 159	87 398	156 557
1971	59 873	137 608	197 481
1972	59 162	260 007	319 169
1973	44 516	316 438	360 954
1974	24 357	207 561	231 918
1975	11 170	115 718	126 888

Source: 1965–1970 – Central Statistical Office (1974) *Annual Abstract of Statistics, 1974.* No. 111. HMSO.

    1971–1975 – Department of the Environment (1976) *Housing and Construction Statistics.* No. 17. HMSO.

improvements and conversions. Not until 1970 can any noticeable increase be identified (Table 9.4). From 1970–74, rehabilitation took place at a rate not previously experienced in England and Wales. The peak was reached in 1973 since when the rate has declined so that rehabilitation is currently running at a level similar to that of the early 1960s.

The moderate upturn in 1970 clearly resulted from the passage of the 1969 Housing Act. The major upsurge in 1972 presumably reflects the combination of 'natural' growth and the even more favourable conditions available under the Housing Act, 1971, in development and intermediate areas. No doubt the progress in the early 1970s also benefited from the publicity given to the campaign in 1972. 'Even before the Housing Act became law in 1969, it was appreciated that better improvement grants would not alone bring about a nation-wide improvement boom. Publicity and practical help were essential too. . . .' (Morton, 1972a, p. 517.) This was provided at an official level by local publicity campaigns and by the publication, in June 1972, of two Government booklets – *Environmental Design* and *House Improvement and Conversions.*

    Given the increased publicity and practical information that attended the rehabilitation programme in the early 1970s, perhaps the reduction in renovation activity is somewhat surprising. One of the first commentaries on the phenomenon was a short feature by Bradney (1973, p. 1 017). In it, the author cited several possible explanations for the reduction in improvement activity. In retrospect, perhaps the most relevant were:

(i) councils were clamping down on grant applications from housing speculators;
(ii) councils were waiting for the outcome of the inquiry by the House of Commons Expenditures Committee into house improvement grants;
(iii) people were not applying for grants because of the shortage of builders owing to a shift within the building industry away from improvement work.

Certainly the Housing Act of 1974 brought about a general tightening up in the allocation of improvement grants but perhaps of even greater significance to the whole rehabilitation programme was the political and economic uncertainty of the period. Undoubtedly, the initial progress under the 1969 Housing Act was retarded by the fact that a general election was held within twelve months of the Act being passed. This brought about a change in Government and the Conservative Party remained in power until March 1974 when a Labour Government was elected. Six months later, after a further general election, the Labour Party was re-elected but with an overall majority of only five seats. Such conditions did not generate the confidence and stability necessary for positive, dynamic government and rapid progress. What is more, the early 1970s were marked by a gradual worsening of Britain's economic position, chronic inflation and massive cuts in public expenditure. Naturally, housing policy did not escape these developments. Early in 1975, for instance, the Government announced that spending on improvement must fall to £280 million in 1975–76 from the 1974–75 level of £450 million. Such cuts were explained by the Minister for Housing and Construction who argued that, in a time of financial constraint, the Government had to reduce spending on less-essential renovation. Although it was recognised that this would lead to serious problems in many areas, the Government was 'determined to get the priorities right in this task of renewing the nation's substandard housing' (Freeson, 1975, p. 2 012). This cut in public expenditure certainly resulted in a reduction in the rate of rehabilitation (Table 9.4) but there can be little doubt that it was somewhat clumsily executed and did not necessarily achieve its desired effect. The cut was not selective – it was not focused on authorities with large programmes of 'less-essential' renovation – and authorities were not given adequate warning. As a consequence, many authorities would undoubtedly have been committed to projects which, in the Government's view, were unnecessary. Since, as Morton (1975) has observed, the sums received by the various authorities tallied almost exactly with the sums already committed by contract, it is inevitable that, in many instances, the less essential renovation was undertaken at the expense of the essential.

In spite of these various setbacks, it is possible to regard the rehabilitation drive initiated by the 1969 Housing Act as a national success. Not only did the annual number of improved dwellings increase, but considerable inroads were made into the stock of 4.5 million dwellings which, in 1967, had been identified as requiring renovation. In the seven years from 1969 to 1975, 1.5 million dwellings were repaired and improved. What is more, the programme successfully effected a swing towards 'full modernisation'. Prior to 1969, as Table 9.4 reveals, the standard grant for basic amenities accounted for over 50 per cent of all improvement grants. After the 1969 Housing Act had been passed, the number of discretionary grants increased considerably so that, in 1975, discretionary grants accounted for approximately 91 per cent of all grants given.

When the figures are examined regionally, several interesting features emerge. Table 9.5 describes the housing situation in 1967 by planning region and examines the regional distribution of improvement grants since 1969. It reveals that progress was greatest in the three northern planning regions in which occurred the greatest proportion of unfit dwellings. The rate of improvement in the south-east appears to have been well below that which might have been expected, given the region's share of both the country's dwelling stock and substandard properties. This is somewhat surprising. Commenting on the progress up to 1971, Morton (1972b, p. 118) observed that 'the tide is clearly rising right across the country, but it is not rising any more – and in some instances is rising less – in the worst affected areas. The three northern regions together barely got their share, netting 33 per cent of the grant approvals for their 31 per cent of the stock.' Presumably the change since 1971 reflects the impact of the measures taken

Table 9.5 Grants approved and characteristics of the dwelling stock by region, 1969–1975

PLANNING REGIONS	GRANTS APPROVED 1969–1975	DWELLINGS LACKING ONE OR MORE OF THE BASIC AMENITIES	ALL DWELLINGS 1967
	%	%	%
Northern, North West Yorkshire and Humberside	45.6	35.5	32.0
South-east	20.4	28.6	33.9
Rest of England and Wales	34.0	35.9	34.1
All of England and Wales	100.0	100.0	100.0

Source: Ministry of Housing and Local Government (1968b) and Department of the Envirironment *Housing and Construction Statistics* Nos. 8 and 17.

to direct resources to the worst areas, namely the post-1970 local publicity campaigns and, particularly, the preferential subsidies given in the intermediate and development areas under the 1971 Housing Act.

While the rehabilitation drive may be regarded as a qualified numerical success, it must be appreciated that the programme was not successful from every aspect. Loopholes in the legislation, for instance, resulted in grants being used for purposes for which they had not been intended. Reference has been made earlier to the profits made out of the improvement grant programme by property speculators, to the process of gentrification and to grants being used to improve second homes. Government recognition of these problems is evident in the 1974 legislation which, in part, attempted to change the improvement grant system so as 'to give more help towards meeting the needs of those people who find it more difficult than others to provide themselves with a decent place to live' (Department of the Environment, 1973b, p. 1). Work on environmental improvement has also been extremely limited and the General Improvement Area concept did not have the impact originally anticipated. In 1973 the Government admitted that 'general improvement areas have so far failed to raise the standards of our older residential districts to the extent that the Government considers both desirable and possible.' (Department of the Environment, 1973b, p. 5.) Information about the progress of the General Improvement Area programme is collected by the Department of the Environment and published quarterly in *Housing and Construction Statistics*. From August 1969 to December 1974 some 915 improvement areas were declared involving approximately 279 218 dwellings. By the end of 1974 work on only 25 940 dwellings had been completed. However, 74 765 grants had been approved but these formed only 5 per cent of the total number. With the cuts in public expenditure referred to above and the financial incentives of the Housing Act, 1974, progress since December 1974 appears to have increased slightly. Up to the end of the first quarter of 1976 a further sixty-five areas had been declared. Work had been completed on another 12 103 dwellings and although no more than 13 231 grants had been approved, these constituted some 8.5 per cent of the total in England and Wales.

The official figures demonstrate, quite clearly, the failure of the General Improvement Area programme in terms of its overall contribution to the improvement of housing conditions in England and Wales. Based on local authority returns, the official figures are notoriously unreliable and incomplete, however. What is more, the General Improvement Area programme has acquired several additional objectives since the passage of the 1969 Housing Act. This being the case, these additional objectives must be considered in any assessment of the programme. Roberts (1976) attempts to do this in his book *General Improvement Areas*. Basing his observations on a survey of seventy-five sample areas, he attempts to assess the programme not only in terms of its national contribution to the improvement of property, but also in terms of its social impact and its effect on environmental improvement. He comes to the conclusion that the rate of progress was greatest in the public sector. In the private sector only 18 per cent of the dwellings in need had been improved with grant aid and no more than 1.8 dwellings were improved each month, on average. On the basis of his sample, he estimates that the level of success, in terms of the General Improvement Area contribution to national house improvement progress, is higher than the published figures might suggest, but that these special areas only 'achieved about the same amount of progress as the country as a whole' (Roberts, 1976, p. 154).

Considerable variation was found to exist in terms of environmental improvement. Generally progress was slow and frequently it was hindered by difficulties in land acquisition. Where environmental improvements had been carried out, they were found to have been limited to cosmetic improvements such as pedestrianisation and traffic management schemes, the resurfacing of roads and pavements, and the provision of new street lights, parking spaces, etc. A similar conclusion was reached by the Information and Intelligence Unit of the National Community Development Project. In its report on the effects and implications of improvement policies for the people living in eight project areas, the Unit concluded that 'compared with redeveloped areas, even those GIAs where environmental works have been done have fared badly. There is no money for community facilities.' (National Community Development Project, 1975, p. 9.) Roberts's observations on the social impact of General Improvement Areas are inadequate. He argues that the vagueness and non-explicit nature of the goals makes it impossible to measure the degree of movement towards them. While the social objectives of the improvement area concept may not be stated explicitly, the social objectives of rehabilitation are and the CDP Information and Intelligence Unit examines the performance of the GIAs in the light of these. It concludes that 'the policy has worked to the advantage of the better-off owner-occupier. For those without capital it has been of little value, and for tenants even less . . . in some areas landlords have been better able to realise their investment and sell rented houses which became vacant. Combined with the decline in council housebuilding, this has forced many people . . . into owner occupation. . . . The break-up of communities has not occurred in any dramatic way. But in several improvement areas resident groups report that there has been a decline over the last six years. And this has led to a decline in their commitment to the area, and thus to a slower, but equally effective, disintegration of the community, because long-standing residents are leaving.' (National Community Development Project, 1975, p. 12.) The logic of the last sentence is confused, but it would appear that the social impact of the

General Improvement Area programme has not necessarily been of benefit to the community.

While the period from 1965 was marked by increased emphasis on house improvement, it was never intended that the rehabilitation programme should replace slum clearance; the overall objective was to stimulate rehabilitation in an attempt to reduce the loss of scarce resources and to avoid the rate at which slum properties were formed. This was made perfectly clear on several occasions. In its programme for 1965 to 1970 (Ministry of Housing and Local Government, 1965), the Government stressed that about one million new dwellings were required to replace slum properties already identified while just under two million were needed to replace old houses not worth improving. The point was re-emphasised in the 1967 White Paper, *Old Houses into New Homes,* which argued that 'as more and more new houses are built more unfit old houses ought to be cleared. And the number to be cleared has been underestimated in the past.' (Ministry of Housing and Local Government, 1968a, p. 9.) Admittedly, a noticeable change in emphasis had occurred by 1973. By this date many of the social implications of clearance outlined in Chapter 5 were becoming apparent and the Government was beginning to appreciate the problems involved. As a consequence, it came to the conclusion that 'in the majority of cases, it is no longer preferable to attempt to solve the problems arising from bad housing by schemes of widespread, comprehensive rede-velopment.' (Department of the Environment, 1973b, p. 4.) This did not mean that the clearance programme had been abandoned. Rather, the Government intended that the worst properties should be cleared and redeveloped, while others should be given minor improvement and repair pending clearance in the medium term. Only the sounder properties would be substantially improved. This concept of gradual renewal, first introduced in the mid-1950s, requires that at any point in time, the worst housing conditions will be remedied by clearance.

As Table 9.6 reveals, the rate of slum clearance actually increased over the period reaching an all-time high in 1968. Only in 1974 and 1975 did the number of dwellings closed or demolished fall to below the level of the main slum clearance drive of the late 1950s and early 1960s. Presumably this decline reflected the influence of the general cuts in public expenditure and the 1973 shift in emphasis outlined above.

CONCLUSION

The failure of the British Government to solve the problem of slum properties can be attributed to several factors. In the first place, there is the strategy employed. For much of the period, the Government was concerned with alleviating the symptoms rather than remedying the cause. Doubt may remain over the question of whether policies have ever been directed at the cause of the problem. This will be examined in more detail in the next chapter. For the present it is sufficient to point out that recent years have witnessed an increasing awareness of the problems on the part of the Government and the policy of slum eradication has been combined with one of slum prevention. The full effectiveness of this strategy has been limited, however, by the political and economic uncertainties of the period. Second, there is the mechanism by which the strategies have been implemented. Given the structure of housing management in Britain, the local authorities are responsible for implementing the policies devised by the central Gov-ernment. The early legislation failed because it embodied neither compulsion nor incentive. The lack of any financial inducement meant that the cost of improvement had to be paid out of the rates which in the poorer areas (where the problem was frequently

Table 9.6   Slum clearance in England and Wales, 1965–1975

	DWELLINGS CLOSED OR DEMOLISHED	PERSONS MOVED
1965	60 666	171 595
1966	66 782	177 283
1967	71 152	185 132
1968	71 586	188 895
1969	69 233	173 447
1970	67 804	169 598
1971	70 057	157 125
1972	66 098	148 338
1973	63 557	132 703
1974	41 698	96 193
1975	49 083	117 183

Source: Ministry of Housing and Local Government *Housing Statistics* and Department of the Environment *Housing and Construction Statistics*.

most acute) only intensified the poverty of the community. Even when subsidies were given, authorities differed in the level of their commitment. As Sigsworth and Wilkinson (1972–73, p. 140) discovered in their investigation of the various constraints on the uptake of improvement grants 'the attitudes of leading authority officials directly concerned in the implementation of improvement grant policy – attitudes which presumably reflect in varying degree those of the local politicians who are ultimately responsible – contributed substantially to variations in the uptake of grants.' Adamson (1974) is even more specific in her survey of local authority procedures for implementing housing improvement policies. She concludes that 'the take-up of housing improvement grants has tended to be greater in . . . Conservative dominated councils than in Labour dominated councils. . . .' (Adamson, 1974, p. 384.) Clearly policies should be interpreted in terms of local conditions, but if, as Sigsworth and Wilkinson (1972–73) suggest, local authorities rarely have an overall strategy towards their older houses and there is a need for the education of local authority officials, perhaps the implementation of central Government policies should not be left to the local authorities. What is more, it would appear that until the late 1960s central Government policies failed to recognise the variable nature of the housing problem and failed to provide adequate stimulus for those authorities in which the problem was most severe.

CHAPTER 10
CONCLUSION

The previous chapters have outlined the problem of slum housing and have examined many of the difficulties surrounding the implementation of potential solutions. In theory, the problem can be resolved relatively simply by eradicating all known slums and preventing other accommodation from becoming obsolete. It is clear from the evidence available, however, that the solution is more difficult to achieve in practice than it is in theory. As the previous chapters have demonstrated, attempts to meet these two objectives have not only failed but have often generated further problems.

SLUM ERADICATION

Inevitably the eradication of slum housing requires that the worst properties are demolished. Equally inevitably demolition has generated further serious problems, mainly of a social nature. For clearance policies to have even the remotest chance of success, alternative housing has to be provided. Invariably this requires that the tenant moves to another locality, places considerable emotional strain on both the household and the community and involves the resident in increased expenditure. What is more, clearance programmes rarely bring about any reduction in the social problems of the slum and not infrequently the point has been made that renewal programmes merely transfer the slum from one area of the city to another.

Because of the apparent failure of renewal programmes, recent years have witnessed the emergence of alternative strategies for dealing with the problems of slum housing. For instance, there appears to be increasing support for what Harvey (1973, p. 144) calls the philosophy of 'benign neglect'. Support for this has come from the general social trend towards the rights of the individual. It is argued that if the under privileged are permitted to remain in cheap housing, they are spared the increased costs inevitably incurred with newer housing and are able to allocate their incomes as they think fit, not as someone else believes they should. So, although the underprivileged remain poor, they 'have one of the luxuries of the rich: control over their own lives' (Ravetz, 1975, p. 73). Clearly this is in direct opposition to the traditional belief that the underprivileged should not be deprived of the right to live in good-quality, modern housing. Accordingly, recent housing policy has witnessed the emergence of two conflicting themes. As Ravetz (1975, p. 71) has observed, modern housing policy displays a distinct conflict between 'the urgent need to give people decent homes and the degree to which policies of clearance and rehousing are, in fact, instruments of oppression'. Rather strangely, both policies are based on the concept of social justice and the belief that the underprivileged should have the same opportunities as their more fortunate counterparts.

An alternative strategy is the elimination of poverty. In 'The failure of urban renewal', Gans (1965, p. 36) argues that 'a standard dwelling unit can make life more comfortable, and a decent neighbourhood can discourage some antisocial behaviour, but by themselves, neither can effect radical transformations. What poor people need most are decent incomes, proper jobs, better schools and freedom from racial and class discrimination.' Given these opportunities, Gans claims, people would be able to leave the slums 'under their own steam'. The weakness of the argument lies in the concept of poverty. Gans sees the poverty of the slum dweller largely in terms of finance and opportunity. In reality, many slum dwellers lack not only the opportunity and the financial resources to escape from poor housing, but also the physical and mental resources. Even with appropriate financial aid, many slum dwellers would not be able to organise their resources to enable them to escape from the slum. What is more, as the literature on slum clearance demonstrates, many slum households have difficulty adjusting to new environments and most keep up the values and life-styles of the slum long after relocation has taken place. What the majority of slum dwellers require is encouragement, guidance, advice and assistance.

While there may be valid philosophical and theoretical reasons for 'benign neglect', it can be argued that the practical objections to renewal are little more than rationalisation. Clearance and rehousing policies have failed because attention was focused on the renewal of buildings and not the renewal of people. If the problems of the slum are to be eradicated, more attention will have to be paid to the needs of the residents. As Gans (1965, p. 36) observes 'the ideal approach is one that coordinates the elimination of slums with the reduction of poverty.' However, it must be appreciated that the term 'poverty' includes not only the financial inadequacies of the slum dweller, but also the personal and social inadequacies that are all too frequently characteristic. While it might be tempting to believe that the social problems of the slum will disappear once the economic problems are removed, this attitude is as naive as the now discredited belief that better housing will produce better citizens. Admittedly, increased prosperity will almost certainly produce an all-round improvement in the quality of life, but it is just as wrong to assume a causal relationship between poverty and the social problems of the slum as it is to assume that these problems are caused by bad housing. Certainly many slum dwellers are poor, but the poverty of the slum is not simply the poverty of unequal opportunity. Rather, it is the poverty of personal and social resources. Renewal programmes should attempt to eliminate the total poverty of the slum; that is the poverty of personal and social resources as well as the poverty of income and residential accommodation. Schemes for the renewal or rehabilitation of residential areas must be combined with schemes for the renewal and rehabilitation of people. They must strive to reduce the trauma of the renewal/rehabilitation process and attempt to equip the household mentally, socially and economically for life in its new or rehabilitated environment.

REDUCING OBSOLESCENCE

Attempts to reduce the rate of physical obsolescence in housing have been equally unsuccessful. As was pointed out in Chapter 3, a dwelling can be regarded as being obsolete if the physical condition of the property renders it unsuitable for continued occupation and if the amenities provided by the dwelling and its environment are inadequate to meet the needs of the occupants. Clearly, the life of a property can be

prolonged by maintenance work which is properly planned and executed. Unfortunately, this is all too rarely the case, particularly in the homes of the urban poor.
Frequently, the occupants lack the economic and personal resources necessary for the
effective maintenance of the property, and, while private landlords tend to be more
concerned with short-term profits than with the preservation of a capital asset, public
landlords (certainly in Britain) rarely have the financial reserves necessary to maintain
their older dwellings. As a consequence, dwellings deteriorate physically as a result of
tenant use and the effects of the elements. To retard the rate of physical decay, the
Government must ensure that its stock of dwellings is properly maintained. At the same
time, new building styles and materials must be developed which minimise the need for
costly and frequent maintenance.

Efforts to offset social or functional obsolescence have involved the introduction of
minimum design standards. Such efforts have not been entirely successful. In the first
place, the adoption of minimum standards works against the provision of low-cost
housing. The property provided is too expensive for the urban poor, and complex
subsidies and rent rebate schemes have to be introduced to ensure that the accommodation can be occupied by the households for which it was intended. Such schemes are
unwieldy to administer and costly to finance. Not infrequently, poor design and inferior
materials and construction techniques are used in an attempt to reduce cost. In Coventry
(England), for instance, it has been found that:

> In the larger blocks efficient expansion joints are omitted and cracks occur in the
> rendering and even the wall fabrics. On the Wood End and Willenhal Estates (and
> possibly others) shale rather than hardcores had been used as a base. Swelling has
> occurred when this has expanded in contact with subsoil water. In some cases the
> damp proof membranes have been penetrated and moisture can enter rooms. Many
> tenants complain that party walls are too thin, privacy is impossible and neighbour
> relations are aggravated. (Coventry Community Workshop and Shelter, 1973,
> p. 7.)

These conditions were discovered in property constructed after 1945 but it is not
unusual for such faults to become apparent shortly after the property is completed and
occupied for the first time. The result is not only the need for costly alteration, repair and
maintenance work but also considerable tenant dissatisfaction and, often, premature
closure. Recently there has been a move in Britain to reduce costs by building to a
reduced standard. Since 1969, all public sector housing in Britain has been built to
'Parker Morris' standards. Recommended some eight years earlier, the standards were
obsolete long before they were generally adopted. Even so, several local authorities are
now building at standards somewhat below Parker Morris. In Sheffield, for instance,
dwellings are being constructed to the standard adopted by the National House Builders
Council – the standard usually adopted in the private sector. This means lower space
standards and 'a reduced heating provision, no downstairs w.c., and the overall storage
area is less, particularly in the kitchen' (Berry, 1976, p. 70). If the estimates of Sheffield's department of planning and design are correct, it also means a saving over Parker
Morris of about £3 000 per dwelling, and, as Berry (1976, p. 70) observes, 'the savings
mean either lower rents or lower public subventions or more houses or any combination
of the three.' However, there is no consensus over the policy. To some the reduced
standards represent a retrograde step, to others they emphasise the social inferiority of
the urban poor. To anyone who has lived in both types of property one thing is certain.
These reduced standard properties are already socially obsolete and it is clear that little
attention has been paid to the kind of shelter that should be provided and to thinking the
problem out from first principles.

The second reason why the policy of minimum design standards has failed is that the standards themselves have failed to anticipate the social, economic and technological changes that have occurred and the rate at which these changes have taken place. This point has already been made in the conclusion to Chapter 3 where it was observed that in Britain, the standards recommended in 1918 and 1961 by the Tudor Walters and the Parker Morris Committees failed to counteract obsolescence. It would appear that if such standards are to fulfil the purpose for which they were intended (i.e. they must ensure that the property does not become obsolete before its intended life is complete), more rigorous attention needs to be paid to the study of user requirements and to changing patterns of living. In their classic study of user needs, Hole and Attenburrow (1966, p. 2) point out that as dwellings may have to meet the needs of several genera-tions of users, the architect requires not only 'a systematic body of knowledge on user requirements, but also an awareness of social trends'. Even this is not sufficient. If obsolescence is to be retarded more effectively, a more rigorous understanding is required of the process by which the living habits of households are changed and the functional demands placed upon the dwelling are thereby altered.

While prediction has been made more accurate and precise through the develop-ment of sophisticated forecasting techniques and the application of scientific methods of analysis (particularly systems concepts) to behavioural problems, it will be some time before housing standards and design are based on a scientific understanding of change and a full appreciation of future user requirements. In the meantime, alternative solutions have to be found. One, quite obviously, is to reduce the intended life of the property; to construct short-life dwellings. In Britain, this approach was adopted in the years immediately following the Second World War. During the period, many short-life prefabricated dwellings were constructed. These properties had an anticipated life of ten years and were intended as a stop-gap to meet the immediate housing shortage. Unfortunately, the nature and magnitude of the housing problem meant that the majority of these structures had to be used for periods considerably in excess of the period for which they were intended. The problem with short-life building as a solution to the process of obsolescence and decay is that it is not yet possible to predict the period over which a dwelling will be expected to provide accommodation. Accordingly, it seems more prudent to continue building dwellings with a traditional anticipated life-span of sixty years or more.

A further alternative now being adopted by a number of British local authorities is the 'starter' or extendible home. The objective is to provide low-cost residential units which contain the minimum facilities necessary to satisfy the immediate requirements of the household. As requirements change and the financial position of the household improves, so the dwellings can be modified and extended to meet these new user needs. While the effects of these schemes are still being monitored, provisional results (Berry, 1976; Griffiths, 1976) indicate that the schemes are highly successful. Certainly the dwellings appear to be in high demand and to provide a source of high quality, relatively low-cost housing which, in theory at least, can be adapted and modifed so as to retard the rate of obsolescence brought about by changes in household circumstances and social and technological innovation. Many of the properties are 'unfinished' – that is, without floor-tiling, wall-plaster and painting throughout, all timber work simply being primed. This means that costs are further reduced and households are able to 'finish' the property themselves, as and when they are able and according to their own tastes and standards. While many would argue against 'unfinished' housing, it does have the advantage of reducing costs but maintaining standards. In addition, it permits greater variety and gives households the opportunity to be involved in the creation of their own shelters. Such 'self help' solutions are finding favour in the 'sites and services' schemes currently being implemented in many underdeveloped countries. In these countries, the national governments have recognised that 'municipally-built houses are simply too expensive both for the governments that build them and for the poor people that rent them' (Bugler and Black, 1976, p. 14). As a consequence, they have directed their attention and resources to the provision of sites and services. Schemes vary but the basic belief is that given security, encouragement and help, the urban poor will build their own homes and 'if it is their house, created by them in their own way, they will eventually improve it as their own circumstances improve.' (D'Souza, 1976, p. 13.) While such idealistic schemes provide a possible solution to the housing shortage and to the problem of low-cost housing, it is doubtful whether, in isolation, they will emerge as the solution to either the problem of slum housing or the social problems of the slum.

REFERENCES

Adamson, S. (1974) 'The politics of improvement grants', *Town Planning Review,* October, **45,** pp. 375–86.

Allerton, R. J. (1963) 'Subsidised rehabilitation in Britain', *Journal of Housing,* **20,** No. 5.

Anderson, M. (1964) *The Federal Bulldozer: a critical analysis of urban renewal, 1914—1962.* MIT Press.

Bagby, D. G. (1973) *Housing Rehabilitation Costs.* Lexington Books.

Barnes, W. (1974) 'The financial and social costs of urban renewal', *Housing Review,* March/April, **23,** pp. 35–40.

Barresi, C. M. and **Lindquist, J. H.** (1970) 'The urban community: attitudes toward neighbourhood and urban renewal', *Urban Affairs Quarterly,* March, pp. 278–90

Berry, F. (1974) *Housing: the great British failure.* Charles Knight.

Berry, F. (1976) 'Retreat from Parker Morris', *Municipal Review,* **47,** June, pp. 68–70.

Bowley, M. (1945) *Housing and the State, 1919—1944.* George Allen and Unwin Ltd.

Bradney, D. (1973) 'Has the improvement grant bubble burst?', *Municipal Engineering,* **150,** 11 May, p. 1 017.

Bugler, J. and **Black, M.** (1976) 'Calling off the bulldozers', *New Internationalist,* **42,** August, pp. 14–15.

Burnett, F. T. and **Scott, S. F.** (1962) 'A survey of housing conditions in the urban areas of England and Wales, 1960', *Sociological Review,* **10,** March, pp. 35–79.

Butler, E. W. (1976) *Urban Sociology: a systematic approach.* Harper and Row.

Castle, I. M. and **Gittus, E.** (1957) 'The distribution of social defects in Liverpool', *Sociological Review,* **5,** pp. 43–64.

Central Housing Advisory Committee (1944) *Design of Dwellings.* (Dudley Report) HMSO.

Central Housing Advisory Committee (1956) *Moving from the Slums.* HMSO.

Central Housing Advisory Committee (1966) *Our Older Homes: a Call for Action.* (Report of the sub-committee on standards of housing fitness) HMSO.

City and County of Kingston upon Hull (1971) *Interim Report of the Housing Working Party to the Chairman and Members of the Housing and Town Planning Committees.* Unpublished.

Clarke, J. J. (1926) 'Housing in relation to public health and social welfare', *Town Planning Review,* **11,** No. 4, February, pp. 243–72.

Conzen, M. R. G. (1960) *Alnwick, Northumberland: a study in town-plan analysis.* The Institute of British Geographers Publication No. 27.

Coventry Community Workshop and Shelter (1973) *Coventry Council Houses: the new slums.* Shelter.

Cowan, P. (1965) 'Depreciation, obsolescence and ageing', *Architects Journal,* 16 June, pp. 1 395–401.

Crosland, R. (1976) 'Government change gear in their housing policy', *Building Societies Gazette,* **108,** February, p. 118.

Cullingworth, J. B. (1960) *Housing Needs and Planning Policy.* Routledge and Kegan Paul.

Cullingworth, J. B. (1966) *Housing and Local Government in England and Wales.* George Allen and Unwin Ltd.

Darke, R. and **Darke, J.** (1972) 'Sheffield revisited', *Built Environment,* **1,** November, pp. 557–61.

Davis, O. A. (1960) 'A pure theory of urban renewal', *Land Economics,* **36,** pp. 220–6.

Department of the Environment (1972) *Slums and Older Housing: an Overall Strategy.* Circular 50/72, 25 May, HMSO.

Department of the Environment (1973a) 'Housing Survey Reports No. 9'. *House Condition Survey 1971, England and Wales*. DOE.

Department of the Environment (1973b) *Better Homes: the next priorities*. Cmnd. 5339, June, HMSO.

Dickenson, J. P. and **Clarke, C. G.** (1972) 'Relevance and the "newest geography" ', *Area*, **4**, No. 1, pp. 25–7.

Downs, A. (1969) 'Housing the urban poor: the economics of various strategies', *American Economic Review*, September, pp. 646–51.

D'Souza, B. (1976) 'The house that Raj Kumar built', *New Internationalist*, **42**, August, pp. 12–13.

Duncan, T. L. C. (1971) *Measuring Housing Quality: a study of methods*. Occasional Paper No. 20, Centre for Urban and Regional Studies, University of Birmingham.

Dunham, H. W. (1937) 'The ecology of functional psychoses in Chicago', *American Sociological Review*, **2**, pp. 467–9.

Elks, J. (**1972**) **'Urban renewal'**, *Architect and Surveyor*, **17**, May/June, pp. 9–12.

English, J. and **Norman, P.** (1974) *One Hundred Years of Slum Clearance in England and Wales — Policies and Programmes, 1864—1970*. Discussion Paper No. 1, Department of Social and Economic Research, University of Glasgow.

English, J., Madigan, R. and **Norman, P.** (1976) *Slum Clearance: the social and administrative context in England and Wales*. Croom Helm.

Eversley, D. (1967) 'Life, leisure and houses', *Architects Journal*, pp. 1 337–9.

Eyles, J. D. (1974) 'Social theory and social geography', in Board, C., Chorley, R. J., Haggett, P. and Stoddart, D. R. (eds.), *Progress in Geography*, **6**. Edward Arnold.

Fisher, E. M. and **Winnick, L.** (1951) 'A reformulation of the filtering concept', *Journal of Social Issues*, pp. 47–58.

Foote Whyte, W. (1943) *Street Corner Society*. University of Chicago Press.

Ford, J. (1936) *Slums and Housing: history, conditions, policy*. Harvard University Press.

Freeson, R. (1975) 'Housing Act, 1974', *Municipal Engineering*, **152**, 24 October, pp. 2 011–2.

Fried, M. (1963) 'Grieving for a lost home', in Duhl, L. J. (ed.), *The Urban Condition*. Basic Books.

Fried, M. and **Gleicher, P.** (1961) 'Some sources of residential satisfaction in an urban slum', *Journal of the American Institute of Planners*, November, pp. 305–15.

Friedman, L. M. (1967) 'Government and slum housing: some general considerations', *Law and Contemporary Problems*, Spring, pp. 357–70.

Gans, H. J. (1965) 'The failure of urban renewal: a critique and some proposals', *Commentary*, **39**, No. 4, April, pp. 29–37.

Gauldie, E. (1974) *Cruel Habitations: a history of working-class housing, 1780—1918*. George Allen and Unwin Ltd.

Gee, D. (1974) *Slum Clearance*. Shelter.

Glass, R. and **Frenkel, M.** (1946) 'How they live at Bethnal Green', *Contact: Britain West and East*. Contact Publications Ltd.

Gray, F. (1976) 'Selection and allocation in council housing', *Transactions of the Institute of British Geographers* (New Series), **1**, No. 1, pp. 34–46.

Gray, P. G. and **Russell, R.** (1962) *The Housing Situation in 1960*. Central Office of Information.

Griffiths, P. (1976) 'Alternative housing', *Municipal and Public Services Journal*, 29 October.

Grigsby, W. G. (1963) *Housing Markets and Public Policy*. University of Pennsylvania Press.

Gruen, C. (1963) 'Urban renewal's role in the genesis of tomorrow's slums', *Land Economics*, August, pp. 285–91.

Guy, D. C. and **Nourse, H. D.** (1970) 'The filtering process: the Webster Groves and Kankakee cases', *Papers and Proceedings of the American Real Estate and Urban Economics Association*, **5**, December, pp. 33–49.

Haas, J. H. (1962) *3R's of Housing — a Guide to Housing Rehabilitation, Relocation Housing, Refinancing*. Washington, D.C.

Harrison, J. (1972) *Reprieve for Slums*. Shelter.

Hartman, G. W. and **Hook, J. C.** (1956) 'Substandard housing in the U.S.: a quantitative analysis', *Economic Geography*, **32**, April.

Hartmann, C. (1964) 'The housing of relocated families', *Journal of the American Institute of Planners*, **30**, pp. 266–86.

Harvey, D. (1973) *Social Justice and the City*. Edward Arnold.

Hemdahl, R. (1959) *Urban Renewal*. Scarecrow Press.

Hendy, W. (1970) 'Good business in rehabilitation', *Journal of Homebuilding*, **25**, No. 12.

Hole, W. V. (1959) 'Social effects of planned rehousing', *Town Planning Review*, **30**, July, pp. 161–73.

Hole, W. V. (1965) 'Housing standards and social trends', *Urban Studies,* **2,** No. 2, pp. 137–46.

Hole, W. V. and **Attenburrow, J. J.** (1966) *Houses and People: a review of user studies at the Building Research Station.* HMSO.

House of Commons (1953) *Official Report,* **520,** No. 1, 4 November.

House of Commons (1954) *Official Report,* **535,** No. 9, 10 December.

House of Commons (1955) *Official Report,* **545,** No. 49, 8 November.

House of Commons (1958) *Official Report,* **585,** No. 83, 28 March.

House of Commons (1964) *Official Report,* **691,** No. 76, 18 March.

House of Commons (1972) *Official Report,* **847,** No. 21, 27 November.

House of Commons: Select Committee on Expenditure (1973) *Home Improvement Grants: tenth report from the Expenditure Committee.* Session 1972–73, Paper 349, HMSO.

Hunter, D. R. (1968) *The Slums: Challenge and Response.* The Free Press.

Isaacson, L. (1976) 'Choosing renewal options', *Housing Review,* **25,** January/February, pp. 7–11.

Jacobs, J. (1964) *The Death and Life of Great American Cities. The Failure of Town Planning.* Penguin Books.

Jones, F. M. (1967) 'A study of obsolescence', *Town Planning Review,* **38,** No. 3, pp. 187–201.

Kerr, M. (1958) *The People of Ship Street.* Routledge and Kegan Paul.

Kirby, D. A. (1971) 'The inter-war council dwelling: a study of residential obsolescence and decay', *Town Planning Review,* **42,** No. 3, pp. 250–68.

Kirby, D. A. (1972) 'The maintenance of pre-war council dwellings', *Housing and Planning Review,* **28,** No. 1, pp. 2–7.

Kirby, D. A. (1974a) 'Residential growth: the inter-war years in England and Wales', *Local Historian,* **II,** No. 1, pp. 24–30.

Kirby, D. A. (1974b) 'The modernisation of pre-war council dwellings', *Housing and Planning Review,* **30,** No. 3, July/September, pp. 4 and 5.

Lansing, J. B., Clifton, C. W. and **Morgan, J. N.** (1969) *New Homes and Poor People: A Study of Chains of Moves.* Institute for Social Research, University of Michigan, Ann Arbor.

Lansing, J. B., and **Marans, R. W.** (1969) 'Evaluation of neighbourhood quality', *Journal of the American Institute of Planners,* **35,** No. 3, pp. 195–9.

Lean, W. (1971), 'Housing rehabilitation or redevelopment: the economic assessment, *Journal of the Town Planning Institute,* **57,** No. 5, pp. 226–8.

Lichfield, N. et al. (1968) *Economics of Conservation. York Conservation Study.* HMSO.

Listokin, D. (1973) *The Dynamics of Housing Rehabilitation: macro and micro analyses.* Centre for Urban Policy Research, Rutgers University.

Little, A. D. (1964) *Models for Condition Ageing of Residential Structures.* Technical Paper No. 2, San Francisco Renewal Program.

Local Government Boards for England and Wales and Scotland (1918) *Report of the Committee on the Provision of Dwellings for the Working Classes.* (Tudor Walters Report) Cmnd. 9191. HMSO.

Lonberg-Holm, K. (1933) 'Time-zoning as a preventive of blighted areas', *Architectural Record and Guide,* June.

Lowry, I. S. (1960) 'Filtering and housing standards: a conceptual analysis', *Land Economics,* **36,** pp. 362–70.

Macey, J. P. and **Baker, C. V.** (1973) *Housing Management.* The Estates Gazette.

Maisel, S. J. (1966) 'Rates of ownership, mobility and purchase,' in *Essays in Urban Land Economics.* University of California Press.

Mansell, C. (1972) 'The perpetual housing problem', *Management Today,* January, pp. 76–86.

Marris, P. (1962) 'The social implications of urban redevelopment', *Journal of the American Institute of Planners,* August, pp. 180–6.

Medhurst, F. and **Parry Lewis, J.** (1969) *Urban Decay: an Analysis and a Policy.* Macmillan.

Meyerson, M., Terret, B. and **Wheaton, W. L. C.** (1962) *Housing, People and Cities.* McGraw-Hill.

Ministry of Health (1919) *Manual of Unfit Houses.* HMSO.

Ministry of Health (1921) *Second Annual Report, 1920—21.* Cmnd. 1446. HMSO.

Ministry of Health (1930) *Eleventh Annual Report, 1929—30.* Cmnd. 3667. HMSO.

Ministry of Health (1931) *Twelfth Annual Report, 1930—31.* Cmnd. 3937. HMSO.

Ministry of Health (1933) *Report of the Departmental Committee on Housing.* Cmnd., 4397. HMSO.

Ministry of Health (1934) *Slum Clearance Programmes of Local Authorities, 1933.* Cmnd. 4535. HMSO.

Ministry of Health (1939) *Twenty-first Annual Report, 1938—39.* HMSO.

Ministry of Housing and Local Government (1953) *Houses — the Next Step*. Cmnd. 8996. HMSO.

Ministry of Housing and Local Government (1954) *Housing Repairs and Rent Act, 1954*. Circular No. 55/54 HMSO.

Ministry of Housing and Local Government (1955) *Slum Clearance. Summary of Returns by Local Authorities*. Cmnd. 9593. HMSO.

Ministry of Housing and Local Government (1961) Central Housing Advisory Committee: *Homes for Today and Tomorrow*. (Parker Morris Report) HMSO.

Ministry of Housing and Local Government (1962) *Improvement of Houses*. Circular 42/62. HMSO.

Ministry of Housing and Local Government (1965) *The Housing Programme 1965 to 1970*. Cmnd. 3838. HMSO.

Ministry of Housing and Local Government (1966) *The Deeplish Study Improvement Possibilities in a District of Rochdale*. HMSO.

Ministry of Housing and Local Government (1968a) *Old Houses into New Homes*. Cmnd. 3602. HMSO.

Ministry of Housing and Local Government (1968b) 'House condition survey, England and Wales, 1967', *Economic Trends,* No. 175, May, pp. xxiv–xxxvi.

Ministry of Housing and Local Government (1970a) 'Living in a slum: a study of St Mary's, Oldham', *Design Bulletin* 19, HMSO.

Ministry of Housing and Local Government (1970b) *Moving Out of a Slum: a Study of People Moving from St. Mary's, Oldham*. HMSO.

Mintz, N. L. and **Schwarz, D. T.** (1964) 'Urban ecology and psychosis', *International Journal of Social Psychiatry*.

Mogey, P. M. (1956) *Family and Neighbourhood*. Oxford University Press.

Montero, F. C. (1968) 'Social aspects of rehabilitation', *Building Research,* January–March, pp. 17–21.

Montgomery, D. S. (1960) 'Relocation and its impact on families', *Social Casework,* October, pp. 402–7.

Morris, R. N. and **Mogey, J.** (1965) *The Sociology of Housing Studies at Berinsfield*. Routledge and Kegan Paul.

Morton, J. (1972a) 'Housing', *New Society,* 8 June, p. 517.

Morton, J. (1972b) 'Society at work: improving slowly', *New Society,* 20 January, pp. 118–19.

Morton, J. (1975) 'Conversion cuts', *New Society,* 27 March, p. 789.

National Community Development Project (1975) *The Poverty of the Improvement Programme*. CDP Information and Intelligence Unit, London.

Needleman, L. (1961) 'A long-term view of housing', *National Institute Economic Review,* No. 18, November, pp. 19–37.

Needleman, L. (1965) *The Economics of Housing*. Staples Press.

Needleman, L. (1968) 'Rebuilding or renovation – a reply', *Urban Studies,* **5,** No. 1, February, pp. 86–90.

Nutt, B., Walker, B., Holliday, S. and **Sears, D.** (1976) *Obsolescence in Housing: Theory and Applications*. Saxon House.

Olsen, E. O. (1969) 'A competitive theory of the housing market', *American Economic Review,* September (reprinted in Rasmussen, D. W. and Haworth, C. T. (1973): *The Modern City: readings in urban economics*. Harper and Row).

Osgood, H. N. and **Zwerner, A. H.** (1960) 'Rehabilitation and conservation', *Law and Contemporary Problems,* **25,** No. 4, pp. 705–31.

Pahl, R. (1975) *Whose City?* Penguin Books.

Park, R. E., Burgess, E. W. and **McKenzie, R. D.** (1925) *The City*. University of Chicago.

Pearson, P. and **Henney, A.** (1972) *Home Improvement, People or Profit?* Shelter.

Pepper, S. (1971) *Housing Improvement: goals and strategy*. Architectural Association Paper No. 8. Lund Humphries.

Powell, Christopher (1974) 'Fifty years of progress', *Built Environment,* **3,** October, pp. 532–5.

Ratcliffe, R. V. (1949) *Urban Land Economics*. McGraw-Hill.

Ravetz, A. (1975) 'Housing for the poor', *New Society,* 10 April, pp. 71–3.

Reckless, W. C. (1926) 'The distribution of commercialised vice in the city: a sociological analysis', *Publications of the American Sociological Society,* **20,** pp. 164–76.

Roberts, J. T. (1976) *General Improvement Areas*. Saxon House.

Robertson, J. (1919) *Housing and the Public Health*. English Public Health Series.

Rumney, J. and **Shuman, S.** (1946) *The Cost of Slums in Newark*. Newark.

Schaaf, A. H. (1969) 'Economic feasibility analysis for urban renewal housing rehabilitation', *Journal of the American Institute of Planners,* **35,** No. 6, November, pp. 399–404.

Schmid, C. F. (1960) 'Urban crime areas', *American Sociological Review*, **25**, pp. 527–42 and pp. 655–78.

Scottish Development Department (1968) *Tenements in Rutherglen: a Report on the Housing Condition Survey*. Unpublished.

Scottish Housing Advisory Committee (1967) *Scotland's Older Houses*. HMSO.

Seeley, J. R. (1959) 'The slum: its nature, use, and users', *Journal of the American Institute of Planners*, **25**, No. 1, February, pp. 7–14.

Shaw, C. R. and **McKay, H. D.** (1942) *Juvenile Delinquency and Urban Areas*. University of Chicago Press.

Sigsworth, E. M. and **Wilkinson, R. K.** (1967) 'Rebuilding or renovation', *Urban Studies*, **4**, No. 2, June, pp. 109–22.

Sigsworth, E. M. and **Wilkinson, R. K.** (1972–73) 'Constraints in the uptake of improvement grants', *Policy and Politics*, **1**, No. 2, pp. 131–41.

Smith, D. M. (1971) 'Radical geography – the next revolution?', *Area*, **3**, No. 3, pp. 153–7.

Smith, W. F. (1966) 'The income level of new housing demand', in *Essays in Urban Land Economics*. University of California Press.

Stokes, C. J. (1962) 'A theory of slums', *Land Economics*, **48**, No. 3, August, pp. 187–97.

Suttles, G. (1968) *The Social Order of the Slum: ethnicity and territory in the inner city*. University of Chicago Press.

Timms, D. W. G. (1965) 'The spatial distribution of social deviants in Luton, England', *The Australian and New Zealand Journal of Sociology*, **1**, pp. 38–52.

Tucker, J. (1966) *Honourable Estates*. Gollancz.

United Nations (1967) *Methods of Estimating Housing Needs*. Studies in Methods, Series 7, No. 12.

Walker, M. (1938) *Harvard City Planning Studies*. Harvard University Press.

Warren, M. (1965) 'Conservation and rehabilitation', *Michigan University Law Review*, **63**, No. 5.

Watney, J., Waymouth, N. and **Bradshaw, G.** (1965) *The Gorbals, 1965: an Investigation into the Housing and Social Conditions of the Gorbals and Adjacent Slum Areas of Glasgow*. Christian Action.

Watson, C. J. (1974) 'The housing question', in Cherry, G. E., *Urban Planning Problems*. Leonard Hill.

White, H. C. (1971) 'Multipliers, vacancy chains and filtering in housing', *Journal of the American Institute of Planners*, March, pp. 88–94.

Whittick, A. (1974) *Encyclopaedia of Urban Planning*. McGraw-Hill Book Company.

Wilkinson, R. and **Sigsworth, M.** (1963) 'A survey of slum clearance areas in Leeds', *Yorkshire Bulletin of Economic and Social Research*, **15**, May, pp. 25–51.

Wilkinson, R. and **Talbot, V.** (1971) 'An investigation of the attitudes of families rehoused from slum and twilight areas in Batley, Leeds and York', *Social and Economic Administration*, **5**, October, pp. 236–62.

Wilson, H. and **Womersley, L., Scott Wilson Kirkpatric and Partners** (1969) *Teesside Survey and Plan, Final Report to the Steering Committee*. II, HMSO.

Wingo, L. (1966) 'Urban renewal: a strategy for information and analysis', *Journal of the American Institute of Planners*, **32**, pp. 144–8.

Woolf, M. (1967) *The Housing Survey in England and Wales, 1964*. HMSO.

World Health Organization (1967) *Appraisal of the Hygienic Quality of Housing and its Environment*. Technical Report Series, No. 353. World Health Organization.

Yeates, M. H. and **Garner, B. J.** (1971) *The North American City*. Harper and Row.

Young, M. and **Willmott, P.** (1962) *Family and Kinship in East London*. Penguin Books.

INDEX

(All Acts of Parliament and Legislation listed are British unless marked (US) = American)

Amenities, housing, 64, 65, 76, 84, 90
American Public Health Association, 17
Appraisal of the Hygienic Quality of Housing and its Environment (WHO), 23
Artisan's and Labourers' Dwelling Act (Torrens Act) (1868), 69, 70
Artisans' and Labourers' Dwellings Improvement Act (1875), 70

Batley (Yorks), 38, 39
'benign neglect', 89, 90
Bethnal Green, 10
Better Homes: the Next Priorities (Government White Paper), 75
Birmingham, 51, 65, 80, *Table 7.1*
Boston (Mass. USA), 9–10, 36, 40, 52
    Rehabilitation Programme, 52

Cardiff, 66
Central Housing Advisory Committee: (1944), 40
    Sub-Committee on Standards of Fitness for Habitation (1946), 63
        (1956), 39, 40
        (1966), 14, 16, 60, 61
Central Housing Advisory Sub-Committee, on Standards of Housing Fitness, (1965), 14
Chicago, 52
clearance, 29, 34, 78, 90
    in America, 36–7, 40,
    disruptive effects, 40–6, 87, 89
    effects on rents, 36–7
    in England and Wales, 37–40
    Government policies, 34, 40–1, 69–77, 79, 80, 81
    orders, 71, 81
    programmes, 59, 65, 70–4, 77, 79, 80, 87
    selective, 55
    statistics, *Tables 9.2 & 9.6*
code compliance, 54
compulsory purchase, 41, 43, 71, 73, 81

The Cost of Slums in Newark (Rumney and Schuman), 6
council tenants, 37, 38, 39
Coventry (England), 91
crime, 6

The Deeplish Study: Improvement Possibilities in a District of Rochdale (Ministry of Housing and Local Government), 20
delinquency, 6
demolition, 29, 30, 34, 69, 73, 77, 79, 80, 81, 89
Dennington Committee, x, 60, 74
dwellings, obsolete *see* obsolescence of housing
The Dynamics of Housing Rehabilitation (Listokin) 47

Economic Trends (Ministry of Housing and Local Government), 62
The Economics of Housing (Needleman), 52
Encyclopaedia of Urban Planning (Whittick), 3
environmental conditions, 17, 23, 74, 75, 85, 86, 90, *Tables 2.1 & 2.3*
Environmental Design (Government booklet), 83

Family and Kinship in East London (Young and Willmott), 10
filtering, 26, 29–33
    in Britain, 29
    policy, 69–71
    process, 29–31, 33
    in USA, 29, 31–2
First World War, effects of, 79
flytippers, 43

General Improvement Areas, 75, 76, 85, 86
    social impact, 86–7
General Improvement Areas (Roberts), 86

gentrification, 50, 51, 85
Glowshire Property Co., 51
Government spending, 84, 85
grants, discretionary, 48, 64, 73, 75, 84; *see also* improvement grants
grants, standard, 48, 75; *see also* improvement grants

Home Improvements, People or Profit (Pearson and Henney), 50–1
Homes for Today and Tomorrow (Parker Morris Committee), 28
Honourable Estates (Tucker), 39
House Condition Index, 20
House Condition Survey (1967), 74, 75
House Improvement and Conversions (Government booklet), 83
House Purchase and Housing Act (1959), 64, 73
Houses — the Next Step (Government White Paper 1953), 72
housing, 13–23
    extendible home, 92
    filtering, 26, 29–33
    indexes of unfitness, 16–23
    loans for, 73, 74
    low cost, 91
    maintenance, 25–6
    obsolescence, 24–8, 77; *see also* obsolescence of housing
    quality from rehabilitation, 51
    'self help' schemes, 93
    shortage, 70, 72, 77, 79
    standards, 13–16, 63, 73, 91
Housing (Government White Paper 1963), 73
Housing, the Great British Failure (Berry), 78
Housing, Town Planning, etc. Bill (1908), 38
Housing, Town Planning, etc. Acts
    (1909), 70
    (1919), 70
Housing Acts
    (1923), 29, 70
    (1924), 29
    (1930), 4, 29, 34, 59, 63, 71, 80
    (1936), 63
    (1949), 64, 72, 73
    (1957), 14, 15, 63, 64, 65, 73
    (1964), 64, 74, 75
    (1967), 74
    (1969), 15, 64, 75, 77, 83, 84, 86
    (1971), 75, 83
    (1974), 76, 77, 83–4, 86
Housing Acts (US)
    (1937), 4
    (1949), 34
Housing Action Areas, 76
housing associations, private, 74, 75
Housing and Construction Statistics (Department of the Environment), 85
Housing Defects Index, 17, 23

Housing and Environmental Deficiency, Survey of, 20, 23
Housing (Financial Provisions) Acts
    (1933), 29, 71, 72
    (1958), 48, 73
Housing (Improvement Grants) (Expenses) Regulations, 72
Housing Markets and Public Policy (Grigsby), 31
Housing Needs and Planning Policy (Cullingworth), 73
The Housing Programme, 1965 to 1970 (Government White Paper), 74
Housing Repairs and Rents Act (1954), 59, 63, 64, 73
Housing (Rural Workers) Act (1928), 70
Housing Subsidies Act (1956), 73
Housing of the Working Classes Act (1890), 70
Hull, 38, 39
Humberside, 67, 85, *Table 9.5*
Hyde Park (Sheffield), 41

Ill Health, 6, 70
improvement and conversion, 55, 74, 75, *Tables 9.3 and 9.4*
improvement grants, 48, 70, 72, 73, 74, 77, 83, 84, 88
    discretionary, 48, 64, 73, 75, 84
    misuse of, 85
    preferential, 76
    repair-only, 76
    standard, 48, 75
    variable, 75, 76
Improvement of Houses (Ministry of Housing and Local Government), 73
income, as measure of filtering process, 32
Index of Decay, 17
index of unfitness *see* unfitness, index of
infill development, 55

Kankakee (Illinois), 32

Lancashire, South East, 66
landlords, 26, 91
Leeds, 9, 38, 39, 65, 66, 80, *Table 7.1*
legislation, British, 78–88
    failure of, 87
    local authorities response, 79, 80, 81, 83, 88
Liverpool, 65, 66, 80, *Table 7.1*
Living in a Slum: a Study of St Mary's, Oldham (Ministry of Housing and Local Government), 9
loans for house improvement, 73, 74
Local Government Boards for England and Wales and Scotland (1918), 28
location of slums, 65–68, 77, *Tables 7.1, 7.2 & 7.3*

Macmillan, Harold, 72
maintenance of housing, 25–6, 41, 43, 50, 55, 73, 91
Manchester, 65, 66, 80, *Table 7.1*
Manual of Unfit Houses (Ministry of Health), 63
Measuring Housing Quality (Duncan), 17
mental illness, 6
Merseyside, 66
Midlands, West, 66
minimal rehabilitation, 48
minimum design standards, 91–2
minimum fitness standards, 13, 14–16, 63, 65
    interpretation, 15–16
Ministry of Health Circular to Housing Authorities, 1331 (1933), 59, 71
modernisation, 48, 54

National Community Development Project, 51, 52, 86
necessitarians, permanent, 7
necessitarians, temporary, 7–8
New Homes and Poor People (Lansing, Clifton and Morgan), 31–2
New York, 51
    City Planning Commission, 36
New York State Temporary State Housing Rent Commission, 47–8
Newcastle-upon-Tyne, 43, 66
North-West region, 68, 84, *Table 9.5*
Northern region, 67, 84, *Table 9.5*

Obsolescence of housing, 13, 24–8, 34, 47, 77, 89
    extendible home, 92
    intended life of property, 92
    process of, 25–7
    reduced building standards, 91
    reduction of, 90–3
    types of, 24–5
Old Houses into New Homes (Government White Paper 1968), 15, 61, 75, 87
Oldham *see* St Mary's Ward
opportunists, permanent, 7, 8
opportunists, temporary, 7, 8
Our Older Homes: a Call for Action (Denning Committee), 60
overcrowding, 71, 72, 76

Park Hill (Sheffield), 41
Parker Morris Committee, 28, 91, 92
Philadelphia, 31, 51, 52
policies of governments, 69–77, 78
    clearance, 71–2, 73, 79
    filtering, 69–71
    rehabilitation, 74–6
    subsidies, 70, 71
The Poverty of the Improvement Programme

(National Community Development project), 51
'problem' families, 38–9

Racial factors, 37
reconstruction, economics of, 52
redevelopment, 55, 56
    policy, 69, 70
rehabilitation, 29, 47–56
    in America, 47, 48, 51, 52
    in Britain, 47, 48–9, 82
    definition, 47
    economics, 51–5
    policy, 69, 73, 74–6, 77, 78, 82, 83, 84, 87
    rate of, 83, 84, 86
    renovation, 50
    social aspects, 50–1, 56
    success of, 85, 90
    wreckout, 50
rehousing, 69, 70, 73, 79, 80, 81, 90
relocation, 36, 37, 38
    effect on living costs, 36, 38, 39
    social effects, 40–6, 50
remodelling, 48
renovation, 50, 84
rented accommodation, 31
rents, 36, 37, 38, 73, 91
    effects of rehabilitation, 50, 51
Repair costs, indexes of *see* Scottish Development Department
residential rateable unit, 61
Rochdale, 20
rural slums, 66, 67

St Mary's Ward (Oldham), 9, 37, 38, 39
St Peter's (Newcastle-upon-Tyne), 43
Saltby (Birmingham), 51
satisfactory house, standard for, 63–4
Scotland's Older Houses (Scottish Housing Advisory Committee), 17
Scottish Development Department's Indices of Repair Costs, 20
Scottish Housing Advisory Committee, 17
Second World War, effects of, 72, 80
Sheffield, 41, 91
slum
    attitudes to, 10–12
    definitions, 3–6
    dwellers *see separate entry*
    location, 3, 65–6
    prevention, 87
    problem *see separate entry*
slum dwellers
    categories, 6–8
    effects of residential renewal, 40, 41, 43
    mobility, 8–10
    poverty of, 31, 32, 90
slum eradication, 87, 89–90
slum problem, 59–68, 72, 78

estimates of, 60–2
location, 65–6
magnitude, 59–60, 65
sampling methods, 61–2
standards of suitability for habitation, 63
statistics of, 59–60
surveys, 60–2, 65
The Slums: Challenge and Response (Hunter), 12
Slums and Housing: History, Conditions, Policy (Ford), 4
South-east region, 84, *Table 9.5*
squatters, 43
Standards of Fitness for Habitation (Miles Mitchell Sub-Committee 1946), 14
Standards of Housing Fitness Sub-Committee (1965), 16
standards of suitability for habitation, 63, 65
    minimum fitness standards, 63
    standard for satisfactory house, 63–4
Street Corner Society (Foote Whyte), 5
subsidies for housing, 70, 71, 72, 73, 74, 79, 80
surveys of slum housing, 60–2, 65

Teeside Survey and Plan (Wilson and Womersley), 23, *Table 2.3*
Tenements in Rutherglen: a Report on the

Housing Condition Survey (Scottish Development Department), 20
Torrens Act (1868), 69, 70
Tudor Walters Committee, 27–8, 92
Tyneside, 66

Unfitness, index of, 16–23;
    American Public Health Association method, 17, 18–9
Urban Decay: an Analysis and Policy (Medhurst and Parry Lewis), 17, 20
Urban Land Economies (Ratcliffe), 30

Vandals, 43
vermin, 43
vice, 6

Webster Groves (Missouri), 32–3
World Health Organisation, 23
wreckout, 50

York, 38, 39
Yorkshire, 67, 85, *Table 9.5*
    West, 66